DEDICATION

To Billy Jemison "Preacher", for always showing me the way.

PREFACE

Hello my name is Jasper and I would like to share some of my opinions and experiences with you. I pray that in this book something that I say will not only encourage you, but strengthen you and empower you to go further in your life. We all go through tough circumstances, difficulties, and sometimes we struggle with our lives. At times we all need a word of encouragement. When things seem the darkest I want you to know that the Lord is always with you. He is always with you to omfort you, to lift your spirit, to pull you out of your situation. Don't give in or give up, but be encouraged and press towards your goal. In my life I've been through Polio as a child and other physical difficulties. I've been at a spiritual low and having a self-defeating attitude and low self-esteem, and at one point in my life I found that I was an addict. I struggled with addiction for some forty years- it cost me many opportunities, many jobs, my family, and at one point I thought that my life would never go anywhere. But I want you to know that whatever you're going through- whatever you'd been through- God is with you. When you think your world is falling apart it's actually falling together. Keep faith in the Lord, lift your head up high, and don't worry about life's mistakes. We all make them. I lived an unrighteous lifestyle for many years and the best thing that may have happened to me happened on April 28th, 2009. That's when I had an accident on I-94, broke my neck, and became a quadriplegic. I believe the Lord allowed this to happen to me to bring my lifestyle to a halt, give me time to be still, listen to him, and reflect on my life.

He wanted me to see all the blessings that He had given me all my life. Learn to appreciate my life. Learn to appreciate and accept who I am. This book is filled with words and situations that hopefully will encourage you to keep striving forward. One thing I have learned is that living your life through the word of God is essential. You cannot live a peaceful and happy, joyous life without the Lord. So I pray that reading my words of encouragement will touch you in a way that will cause you to reflect upon your life and see the Lord and what He's done for you. I pray that my words will inspire you, lift you up, and hopefully make you a better person. It is said in scripture that "Fear of the Lord is the beginning of knowledge". So I take that as until you accept Christ in your life, you are blind. The closer you draw to him the closer he'll draw to you, and your eyes shall begin to see new things. My name is Jasper, love and peace be with you.

2011

May 17, 2011

GOD KNOWS

So many of us are walking through this world blind. We go from place to place, we take all kinds of chances with our lives. But God loves us so much that He watches over us whether we believe it or not. If we were living in a world without God you would quickly see the difference. The Father knows what his children need. He provides for those who have lost homes, He heals and mends broken bodies and hearts. He always comes to us baring gifts. For instance, I broke my neck in two places but still He allowed me to live, not only live, He allowed me to keep my right mind. Some folks believe things just happen or they believe in coincidences. I don't. I believe that the Father's always watching over us. Being a quadriplegic gives me time to think about my purpose in life and gives me time to recall a lot of my past experiences and I can see where if I had served the Lord some more I may not be in this situation. It's written that He chastises those who He loves. He took time and slowed me down so I could focus on Him and my life. So if you are going through some turmoil in your life right now I suggest that you just do nothing or find a quite place and meditate on the Lord.

May 17, 2011

TIME

Time is a precious thing. Most of us waste a lot of time doing things that make no sense. Time should be used always in a positive manner. The Lord did not waste time. He rose early in the morning and started his business. He was always seeking to do something meaningful. Can you say that about yourself? Do you waste your time doing childish things or do you spend your time helping others - family and non-family? When was the last time you helped someone you didn't know? Time is a very fleeting thing. It moves on and it will pass you by if you don't use it wisely. In my position, being a quad, I try to be on the move whenever I can. Even though it's a little exhausting I love to stay busy doing my therapy. I look forward to them each day. It lifts my spirit and makes me feel like I'm doing something positive for myself. Take a look at yourself and decide whether or not you use time in a good manner. What do you do to put time to good use?

May 31, 2011

FRIENDSHIP

I have been blessed to have life long friends. People I have met in the course of my life that I've bonded with that we just remained close friends. I believe that friendship is a blessing. I also believe that I am blessed to have more than one life long friend. I have some friends that we've been together over 50 years. It's a blessing to watch each others families grown up. When something happens to me my friends are right there on the spot. We look out for each other, our families and we give each other opinions and advice. If you think friendship is not so important, talk to someone who's never had one. I have noticed through the years some people don't understand the closeness we have, but what can I say, we're like family. And family checks on each other, talks to each other, and tells each other the truth about what they see. I've had friends of all ages, one friend I adopted as my second mother. We've been just that close. I even had one good friend, a co-worker in fact, that we kind of had a disagreement. I didn't curse him, he didn't curse me, but we didn't speak to each other for about a year. Then, one day, by chance, we ran into each other. The friendship started all over. See, if a friendship is true from the beginning, you may go through some bumps, but the friendship is still there. That's because God put it there. I also think a lot of my friendliness comes from my mom. My mother knew somebody everywhere-everywhere she went, she'd make a friend. Some people are so private they cut themselves off from being social. My mother used to say you can't live in this world by yourself.

June 23, 2011

MY LIFE AS A QUADRIPLEGIC

On April 28, 2009 my life came to a turning point. It changed in an instant. My Jeep fell off the down ramp and flipped 2 or 3 times and I broke my neck in two places and from then on my life will never be the same. I went through Intensive Care, after that I went through Rehab for about a month and a half, then I was transferred to where I am now, a Neurocare Center specializing in Spinal Cord Injury. In the beginning I felt alone. I wouldn't come out of my room and participate in any activities. I felt that my life was so limited because I couldn't move. I felt like I could never be the man that I was so I let go of my relationship with my girlfriend. I isolated a lot, but I never forgot what part God played in this. I was warned over and over to change and stop doing the things that I was doing that were negative toward God. I believe that in this injury God saved my life. He is the supreme Father and he chastised me. Slowly I began to change. I started participating in some of the activities they offer. I found that I could do new things. The Lord put me exactly where I needed to be. I take therapy sessions and I have a lot of professional people that really care. If I had to give another quadriplegic any advice the first thing I would say is don't give up on God or yourself. Take a new outlook on life. Life is worth living even in the condition that you are in. Hold your head up and be a man. Your life is not over, it just took another turn and we have to learn to deal with it. It's as simple as that.

July 15, 2011

SOMEPLACE SPECIAL

My name is Jasper and I had a car crash in April 2009, which resulted in me being a Quadriplegic. After having gone through intensive care and Physical Therapy, I landed here at a facility called Special Tree. Actually, my daughters picked it out for me. They said "you'd really like this place". Everyone here is so friendly and it's clean and nice. After I got here I isolated myself- I wouldn't come out of my room for days on end. But this place is more like a huge family rather than just staff. They knew what I was going through and they were very patient with me. I want to focus on a group they have here called Therapeutic Recreation. They urged me time and time again to get out and mingle with the other residents, think of happy things to do, and think of different places to go. Later I discovered it's designed that way to get you back into society. This group (TR) has helped me tremendously. They taught me how to mix and mingle with other people. They even taught me how to laugh again. One thing I'll never forget is the patience and caring they have with me. I go bowling, I play card games and I play family games. Life right now- even though I'm a quad- can still be sweet. So I hope you never find yourself in a position like mine, but if you do, come to Special Tree and they will put your life back together.

August 9, 2011

THEY HAVE FRIENDS. THEY NEED PARENTS.

I remember when I was a kid, growing up it seems like my mother was always just around the corner. She had rules when I was little. A lot of things I couldn't do or places I couldn't go if she didn't know what was there or if it was safe. I remember thinking, "Wow, to be a boy, she keeps a tight leash on me.", but I come to understand she was just doing her job, being a parent. She was always watching out for me. Being a single mother perhaps she was a bit over protective but again I realize that was her job as a parent. I notice this younger generation, they don't have that same nurturing spirit I guess. You could pass through a neighborhood and see 3 and 4 year olds wandering about all by themselves. Even in the house the kids sometimes tell the parents what to do. When I was a kid I wasn't aloud to close my bedroom door because my mother wanted to see what was going on in there, what was I doing. Young parents today don't seem to think that way. A lot of kids are growing up with some of these computers I guess and electronic gadgets. They're not learning to interact with each other. The parents don't take time to teach their kids proper manners. Again, when I was a kid it was "yes ma'am, yes sir" and you learned to stay in a kids place. Now young kids just jump in your conversation as if they're on your level and no one says anything about it. They come and go as they please, as if they're paying rent. I know it seems like a good idea and we do want to be friends with our children growing up, but don't forget they don't need you always as a friend, they need you as a parent. Learn how to stand firm with your decisions and guide them the right way. That's my opinion.

September 1, 2011

LIFE IS TOO SHORT

My name is Jasper and although I'm a quad I attended my high school reunion. It was a beautiful day and also it was a beautiful reunion, getting to see people I hadn't seen in years. My daughters were there along with my grandchildren and it just made for a beautiful family day. I really want to send out this message that if you're crippled, or you are going through some type of rehab and you're thinking that your life is over because you can't do the things you used to do - think again. Life is too short to cut yourself out just because you have a set back. And that's all that is, a set back, because with the technology they have today you can still live a full life but there are some things you have to do. First of all, take an attitude check. Make sure you have a positive, uplifting attitude about yourself, then surround yourself with positive people, doing positive things. The worst thing you could do is be around a bunch of negative, stand still people, never doing anything different. I had a wonderful time at that reunion and two weeks before that I went to a church picnic and I had a wonderful time there and I have no control over my body, but I have tons of support. These are the things you have to do if you can't do things for yourself. You can still live a joyful life. Put yourself in the hands of God and go on living your life. He'll make a way for you. So don't be discouraged. It's not the end of the world, not yet. Put a big smile on your face, take an attitude check and live your life.

September 27, 2011

BE ACTIVE IN THE POLITICAL ARENA BECAUSE IT AFFECTS YOU

My name is Jasper and up till now I've never really thought seriously about what goes on in politics, but now being a quad in a facility, which my auto insurance pays for, I am feeling how seriously this will affect me. There's a Bill that's in the house and a long story short they want to do away with No Fault insurance. This would affect me directly because without the auto insurance I could not maintain the life that I'm living right now. Even if they switched me to Medicaid or Medicare I would not receive the personal attention and care that I get now. They even want to put a ceiling cap on the money that they spend on us. They want to give us, if you are seriously injured, $50,000 to work with. Well if you know anything about the ER or if you have ever stayed in a hospital you know that $50,000 can be spent with one test or one operation. Going through the ER you could spend $50,000. Think very seriously about this Bill because it's going to hurt a lot of poor people if it gets passed so I urge you to get into the political arena and pay attention to what the politicians are trying to do. You may find that it affects you. This is Jasper, may God Bless You! Good bye.

September 29, 2011

DON'T ACCEPT EVERYTHING LIFE THROWS AT YOU

Life can sometimes throw you a curve that seems totally unfair to you but you have to learn to accept certain things and certain things you don't. For instance, there's a Bill that wants to kill No-Fault Insurance. Don't lay down and accept things like this. Rather...fight back any way you can. You may be jobless but you got to keep pressing forward and sooner or later something will open up for you. I've been there, I know. I'm a quad in a rehab. I got through a series of treatments everyday. I believe that one day my body will be strong enough to use some of the limbs I used to have, such as my arms and hands, and perhaps even my legs. I have not just laid down and accepted this situation I'm in. I tried to be as active as I was before the accident. My outlook on life is good. I don't know what I may do next. If you want to give up and wallow in your misery, God will allow you to do that. If you pray and press forward tell Him what you need and He'll provide it for you. You have to believe that. Once again, this is from Jasper Matthews. These are some of my thoughts.

October 13, 2011

A PLACE CALLED SPECIAL TREE

My name is Jasper and I'm a quad and I live at a place called Special Tree. It's a neurological rehab but it looks more like the Ritz Carleton when you come inside. It's a brand new building that was built from the ground up and all the clients moved from the old building to the new. There are paintings on the walls and elaborate clocks and fixtures and sometimes I begin to think that a lot of what was done was done with the clients in mind. Our rooms are bigger, all the beds are new, the grounds are very eye appealing, all the rooms have flat screen TVs. They even put white robes in the bathrooms for the clients. They could have just left it at that, but they also added DVD players. Being a client myself I don't take this building for granted. In my opinion there are a lot of things I see that are designed for the client and I understand they didn't have to do that. They didn't have to put DVD players in the rooms or they didn't have to put so much thought into making this building comfortable. Each room has it's own thermostat. There are a lot of things that I see that are comfortable for us that they didn't have to do. I don't know about you but I'm very happy to be here at Special Tree because I understand there are a lot of places such as this where you're not treated as well, you don't get the patient care that you get here at Special Tree. Sometimes when I get sleepy I get tired of them coming in my room but I understand they're taking blood pressure, rolling me over, checking me. Those are the things that need to be done for a person like me. So I think that Special Tree is a very special place and if you're here as a client or you are a staff member I think you are very fortunate. Just dig a little deeper. This is Jasper and these are my opinions.

October 13, 2011

GO DETROIT!!

I'm not much of a sports fan. I like football and this seems to be a magical season for the Lion's. Imagine not winning one game last year. You were below the basement, but the key is never give up and look where they are today. Undefeated so far! I don't know how far the Lion's are going to go but they are off to a fantastic start. Congratulations to the Lion's!

Also I'm not an avid watcher of baseball but I go ahead and watch the Tiger's. I always make a rule to root for the home town team and I have to say I'm proud of our Tiger's. They were at the bottom for so long and now they are a team to reckon with. You can't just push the Tiger's around anymore. They are playing class A baseball and I congratulate them.

October 25, 2011

FAMILY AND FRIENDS ARE A BLESSING

I recently attended a dinner that my cousin cooked for me. What was so interesting was getting my wheelchair into the house. We had to do some twisting and turning but my family was determined to get me and that wheelchair into the house and to my surprise they did. It was a labor of love because they really wanted me there. I felt blessed because I know there are plenty of people who don't have anyone that care for them like that. They wanted me there and they were gonna get that wheelchair in no matter what. After getting into the house another friend of mine who knows the family took time out of his schedule to come by to see me and bless the house. It felt good being there because I hadn't seen them in so long and their mother cried to see me there. She was filled with emotion. When it came time to go, a second friend of mine had come by to see me and my cousins. He said he wasn't leaving until I left and he didn't. When it came time to leave they pitched in again and tackled that wheelchair. My friends all but manually picked up that chair and turned it around so I could get out of the house onto the porch. The driver of the van did a special thing for me by putting the ramp on the porch rather that the ground and that was special to me because I could not have done it without her doing what she did. And again I had a very special feeling about friends and family. Real friends and family - they just don't let you down. They are there for you when you need. Some of these people I hadn't seen in 20 years. Love never dies. So you are blessed to have some family who you know cares about you. If you may have a friend or two who always come when you are in need you are indeed blessed. This is Jasper and these are my thoughts. Be Blessed.

November 1, 2011

HALLOWEEN

Hello my name is Jasper and I have an opinion concerning Halloween. I'm relieved to see so many parents have decided to do Halloween in a different manner than when I grew up. You have to recognize and understand the times that we're living in are often dangerous. When I was a kid we would go in the streets and go to the all the stores we could and all the houses even if you didn't know the person who lived there. Everything was safe. No one really tried to hurt you in the street or there were no safety pins in the apples or any poison in the candy like it is today. That's the reason that I'm so happy to see that parents have taken an active interest in their child's safety. I've been hearing things such as a parent won't take their child to a house unless they know the person who lives there. I don't hear a lot about going to different stores but rather sometimes your company who will give a Halloween party or someone you do know will host a Halloween party where you can go in and feel safe. My Halloween days are over but it's fun to watch my daughters Halloween their kids. The kids love dressing up in the different costumes, especially the girls who are little princesses on Halloween. So bare in mine what type of world we live in and take your child out and Happy Haunting!

November 17, 2011

LOVE ONE ANOTHER

My name is Jasper and I have a friend who is a Minister and she attended an event where love filled the room. I could just see the joy in her eyes when she spoke about how everyone prayed and hugged each other. This event called for Ministers and Saints from all over the country and from all over the world. It was an awesome event as she told me how people were instructed on how to give forgiveness. She said things that were hidden deep in our hearts were brought out as a result of this spiritual event. I wish I had had an opportunity to be there. It sounded like a good time to cleanse ones heart. This event was held at Ford Field. She said the stadium was packed, letting me know that there are many people seeking spiritual relief. God is the way. There is no other way than by him. If you have an opportunity to go to a spiritual retreat or a conference where love and spirituality will overflow you must attend. You may get there and the Holy Spirit can reveal to you you're not quite as holy as you think. But you have an opportunity right at that time to change, to grow for the better. I believe in these events. It's like going to a counselor. He can only help you if you allow Him to. My name is Jasper and these have been my thoughts. Love you, God bless you and be a blessing.

November 17, 2011

THANKSGIVING

Sometimes I wonder if people really understand what Thanksgiving is all about. I'm sure we all have our own idea about it and this one is mine. Thanksgiving is a time to forgive, it's a time to get closer to your family, your children, your spouse. Thanksgiving is a time to worship. As a matter a fact, He has to come first. Thank the Lord, first of all, for being here. You woke up this morning, but somewhere in the world someone didn't. Thank Him. Thank Him also for keeping you all these years, guiding your steps, opening doors for you, and making your life sweet. Give the Lord thanks for His mercy and grace. We don't deserve what he does for us, but he does it out of his love for us. Thanksgiving is a time to sit back and reflect on your life with friends and family and how fruitful your life has been. You have a lot to be thankful for even if you don't think so, think a little longer.

December 2, 2011

HATS OFF TO SPECIAL TREE

I would like to tell you about the place I live at. It's a neurological injury facility. I've been here now a little over 2 years and I want to speak about the staff. Whenever my friends visit here that's one of the first things they notice is the courtesy of the staff. I feel they do an outstanding job and in their eyesight the client comes first. If something goes wrong with the client they come running because they seem to take it personally if you're hurting. I know when I do things or something's going on with me man, word gets around, and they watch me just to make sure I'm ok. Now I'd like to speak about this beautiful building that we built for Special Tree. It's very lovely and spacious. I especially like the way they blended the colors of the walls and different things. It has a real homey feel and look to it. Once you come into the building you can tell there was a lot of thought put into this building. Judging by the furniture and other little things they have you can also tell money was well spent. and it's not only to make the client comfortable, I feel it was designed for the girls also. I could really appreciate a company like that who thinks about their workers and tries to improve their working conditions. So, my hat's off to you Special Tree. Keep up the good work, because there are a lot of people that need you.

December 23, 2011

CHRISTMAS DAY

Here it is again, Christmas day is upon us. I pray that all is well with your family on this day. I don't know what Christmas day means to you- to some I know it's a chance to go spend a day at your family's house, get drunk on free liquor. I've seen families have a very festive time. Everyone loving everyone, everyone getting along and thanking the Lord. I think of my own family during Christmas day- my girls whom I adore watching how they've grown. Remembering how I used to hold them close to me when they were babies, remembering how I used to just lay my baby on my chest and watch her go to sleep. Now they have babies of their own and it's fun to watch them too. They're loud, they're rude, sometimes they're cruel, but they're always fun to watch. Those are babies- those are children. Let them play and be who they are. So I just want to say have a happy and blessed Christmas day. Remember what Christmas is all about. It's not about gifts, it's not about you, it's not about your big car or even your family, you know it's about Him.

December 29, 2011

THE NEW YEAR

Like a lot of people I look forward to the coming year. Somehow it makes me feel that I'm starting my life all over again. I don't make resolutions because most of us don't keep them anyway but I think that you should think differently with each coming year. Plan some new things, plan a new vacation, make a goal to get a promotion on your job, get closer to family members or friends. In other words, don't let one year be like the previous year. When you have the blessing of seeing a new year come in it's like a blessing from God. He's allowing you to get it right one more time. There are so many different things, new things that you can come up with for the upcoming year. It may surprise even you. I'm a quadriplegic and I have plans for the upcoming year. Do some new things, be outgoing. I don't plan on letting my circumstances keep me from doing something new. So think about it. How do you want to live your life? Doing the same thing year after year or do you want this year to be something different in your life. This is Jasper and these are my thoughts.

2012

January 6, 2012

GOD ALWAYS PLACES YOU RIGHT WHERE YOU NEED TO BE

My name is Jasper and I'm a quadriplegic. When this happened to me through my accident with my Jeep, it changed my life so fast I didn't know what to do. But through the help of my daughters, God guided me to a place called Special Tree. It's a neurological rehabilitation facility. I've been here just a little over 2 years and I've seen some wonderful things happen here. People that have been torn apart, bruised, and almost thrown away, with the help of therapy they lived to get their lives back in some sort of order. I'm saying this because if not you personally you may have a loved one that has been injured in some kind of way, and you may not know about a place like this, but this is right where they would need to be. Receiving therapy, guidance, support from the staff, and it'll all help you to get your life back together. I would like to believe that God guided my daughters to this place for me. I couldn't find it on my own, I couldn't move, so my daughters went scouting for me not knowing anything about a place like this. But God guided them here. If you have a loved one that's injured you may not come to Special Tree, but put them in a place where they specialize in head injuries and paralysis.

February 2, 2012

DO IT FOR SOMEONE ELSE

My name is Jasper and I'm a quad and I have a Minister who visits me once a week religiously. I enjoy her company so much that I introduced her to my best friend who is also a Minister like she is. And they came to visit me today and he brought my oldest brother who usually has a very hard time getting out to visit me. I was really surprised to see him and my heart was filled with a lot of joy. And the four of us sat and we just chatted and disagreed about some things as well as agreed about some things. We talked about religion and current events. It was a very spiritual like meeting and we all enjoyed each others company. So as you go about your daily business I pray that you will think about that. Visit someone you haven't seen in a long time or visit someone that you have never visited. Sit with a senior and have a conversation. You may be surprised what you may learn from them. I guarantee you it will make the other person feel so good inside as well as yourself. So do it for someone else. This is Jasper. Have a blessed day.

February 16, 2012

GOD LOVES YOU

My name is Jasper Matthews and I move around in a wheelchair. I am a believer in God, a follower of Christ and it's so amazing to me sometimes the way things happen in my life. When I sit back and think about it I notice the Lord placing me right where I need to be. There's a Minister and we get together every Thursday and we sit and chat about the Bible or just things in general. She invited me to her church and once a week her Pastor teaches and that's the day that I went. I was well received with a lot of affection and his teaching was outstanding. I really enjoyed it. Also he has to get the prophecy. I was very curious about what he might have to say about me. As he began to prophesied he and his host of Ministers, it was really something to see. They would touch these people and pray over them and most of them were so touched they would fall out, have dizzy spells for a while. It was really something to see. After he had prophesied over a number of people he came over to me and he said some things that really touched me and surprised me. I am a believer and I believe that God works through the Preachers and Pastors that he's called so I don't dispute what the man of God has to say to me. He said through my faith I would get up out of the wheelchair some day. He said I will not stay in this wheelchair because God has work for me to do. Then he surprised me further when he said I was going to preach some day. But through it all I was telling myself that God puts you right where you need to be. He puts you where you need to be so you can hear what he wants you to hear. I know that God loves us and he wants only the best for us and don't worry because he has you right where you need to be even if it's uncomfortable. Just sit still and try to hear what he's telling you. That's the way he teaches you, through actions and words. So don't forget he said he's with you always. I'm Jasper Matthews and I believe.

February 24, 2012

LIVING AS A QUADRIPLEGIC

My name is Jasper and I live my life today as a quadriplegic. Before my accident in April of '09 I was a very active guy. I used to like to visit my daughters often, as well as a host of friends that I have. I used to love to accompany a minister friend of mine and we would go various places, various homes, hospitals, and special visits to friends and pray for them. I also had a job when I lived in Arkansas, and the job required me to be very active. You can imagine how I must have felt with my life coming to a sudden standstill. It was quite a blow for me at first, but slowly I began to adjust because I knew "why get upset over something I can't do anything about?" I'm a big believer that God will always place you where you need to be. He placed me at a very nurturing rehab facility and slowly with the help of the staff I began to feel like a normal person again. They taught me how to mix in with other people again. I learned that if you want the victory you do have to pay some dues. I love to attend my therapy sessions- they urge me to go out into society such as going to the movies, to the mall, and especially family visits. They taught me how to be a whole person again instead of a broken man in a wheelchair. So if you have some type of physical affliction, don't give up! You must press on towards your goal and remember, God always puts you right where you need to be and he gives you the tools to do what you have to do.

So my name is Jasper, and I am a quadriplegic. Have a blessed day.

March 21, 2012

IT'S IMPORTANT

My name is Jasper and at one time in my life I was a pretty active guy. I always went where ever I pleased and could usually do what ever I pleased. Then in April '09 a car accident side lined me. My life as I knew it seemed over but with the help of the staff at the rehab I'm in I began to accept my condition. I also learned that it's very important to first accept your condition, believe in God and yourself and become active. I stay active by writing blogs, going on various trips with the rehab, personal visits to family and friends, I take therapy 5 days a week, I attend certain meetings that they have at the rehab, seminars and the like. It's very important to stay active so you can get used to living in your new life as a quadriplegic or whatever injury you have. Staying active recharges your mind and your people skills. It does not give you time to sit around and throw a pity party for yourself. So my friends, I urge you to put God first, believe in yourself and stay active. It's important!

April 4, 2012

LIVE LIFE ON THE FIRST PEW

Hello my name is Jasper and I'm a quadriplegic and I've learned that no matter what physical state, mental state you may be in we all need to be spiritually fed. Sometimes are lives may take a wicked turn, it may seem a turn for the worst, we may feel like our lives are done for but if we learn to live our lives as if we were seated on the very first pew we can learn new things and live a productive life once again. We need Jesus in our lives if we are going to succeed. This is what I believe and this is what I do. I open my heart to the Lord and when I'm in His house I sit on the very first pew. I don't want to miss a thing. I want to hear every word that he has to speak to me and I also live my life that way, as if I'm still sitting on that very first pew. It helps me in so many ways to keep Him on my mind. It helps me to get along with others, keeps me motivated, keeps me safe knowing He's in my life forever. As best I can as I go throughout my day, I keep my mind on that first pew knowing that God is going to provide all my needs. So I say to you if you have any doubts about yourself, life in general, things may not be going your way, I urge you next time you get to your local church march right in and go right to the front and sit on the first pew. It'll give you a whole new perspective. I'm Jasper and these are my thoughts.

April 17, 2012

WAITING ON GOD

Hi, my name is Jasper and I'm a quadriplegic. I know some people do not believe in divine healing. As a matter of fact you may go through your entire lift and not see it, but still it's there. The Lord said by my stripes ye are healed and that means that he bore all our sicknesses. If you believe strong enough, and it be the Lords will, you could actually heal yourself. I myself am a believer. I have no feelings in my lower body but still I believe that through divine healing someday I will walk. Sometimes if you have something as simple as a headache just quiet yourself and meditate and tell yourself you are not going to receive your headache and the Lord will remove it. I was born in the 50's, which was the Polio era, I was a kid who wasn't supposed to walk. I had braces and crutches but I can remember running down the hallway with the Dr's watching me and applauding me. I was not supposed to be able to walk but instead I became able to run thanks to the Lord. So if you, have any affliction that you don't want keep meditating on it and speak to your body. Tell it to remove itself, then have faith in your higher power that he will remove it in His time. Sometimes the hardest thing to do is to wait on something we want so bad. But the Lord said in His word be anxious for nothing. He also said he will not leave you or forsake you but we have to believe. So I don't know about you but I'm waiting on God. My name is Jasper and these are my thoughts.

May 2, 2012

THE QUADRIPLEGIC IN NA

Hello my name is Jasper and I had to make a lot of adjustments in my life not only being a quad, I'm aslo a recovering addict. My clean date is also the same date as my accident. I recently went to a meeting when I celebrated my 3 years clean. I want you to understand that we may have akward conditions, people still love and embrace us as long as we keep a positive attitude and continue on with our lives, people will support us. I went to that meeting not knowing exactly what to expect, but it turned out to be a beautiful experience. They bought a huge cake, pizza, ice cream and we celebrated and hugged each other and they gave me so much support. It was awesome to me that so many people poured out their love for me. I was touched. So I want you to know that things change in our lives but some things remain the same. Love, caring, support, and God working in our lives. So I said all that to say this, it's very important that we look at life with the same zeal that we had before our tragady. God works through people and he touches hearts and moved people to love us unconditionally. Keep your head up and embrace life boldly and it will work for you just as it's working for me. Love you. I'm Jasper and this was my expereience I've shared with you.

May 15, 2012

ATTITUDE, ATTITUDE, ATTITUDE!

Hi, my name is Jasper and I'm a quadriplegic. Today I went out with a group of people and we planted flowers in vases. It may not seem like much to some people but to someone who is severely injured the task can be very rewarding. I feel that if you're an injured person, if you body's crippled or you have some kind of head injury it's very important you keep your chin up and have a positive attitude about life. Don't look at your circumstance, the condition you're in, rather focus on your recovery and future goals. Your spirit is what enables you to move forward, forgetting the past and boldly facing your future. I enjoy what I did today. Just planting a simple flower or getting out of bed just to go play Bingo or a card game, visit someone, better yet pray for someone in your facility or home. Having that positive attitude and Godly spirit will enable you to do things with zeal. The point I've tried to make is that your life is not over. I go on trips to the movies, to the art institute, fishing, bowling and even attended a dance and I did it all being confined to a wheelchair. Attitude...have a positive attitude and see where it takes you. My name is Jasper and I thank you for reading.

May 23, 2012

EVEN THOUGH YOU ARE A QUAD PROBLEMS STILL EXIST

My name is Jasper and I am a quad and I find myself still having to deal with life's problems. I'm currently being garnisheed and I have to personally look into the matter. I got together with my social worker and we're going to set an appointment with the Friend of the Court. Just because you are a quad life still presents problems that you have to address. There may be times though when you feel helpless. For example; my daughter is in the process of a divorce. I feel somewhat helpless not being able to give her the support I would like to. All I can do is talk to her and give her my advice. I wish I could do more but my condition won't allow it. But I keep a good attitude and realize that I must adapt to the situation. Just because we're quads life doesn't change for us. We have to change for it. Be strong, keep a good attitude and just do the best you can. Good bye, my name is Jasper.

June 6, 2012

STAY ACTIVE, ACTIVE, ACTIVE

Hi, my name is Jasper and I'm a quad, but I don't let that stop me from doing things I want to do or go places I want to go. This week for instance I went to 2 church services, I'm going to the movies this week, also to a wedding this week and then spending Father's Day with my family. You do not have to be limited by your condition, your wheelchair. It has wheels...let them roll! Being active is a vital part of your recovery. It stimulates you, motivates you and just keeps you in touch with the outside world so I encourage you to get out, enjoy the sun while it's shining. People will take to you differently. They see you being active, taking charge of your life, people genuinely want to help you when they see you helping yourself. I believe that to be true in my own life. People are always glad to see me and if they won't come to you, go to them. You can if you want to. This is just a short note to let you know that life for you is not over so be active, active, active. My name is Jasper, good bye.

June 13, 2012

OBSTACLES STILL OCCUR

Hello, my name is Jasper and I am a quad. A dear friend of mine had invited me to his daughters wedding and he told me weeks in advance. But would you know, about a day or two before the wedding we both learned there were no ramps to get into the church. Well the thought of not going never entered my mind. He is a dear friend and our families grew up together. I knew when his daughter was born and there was no way I was going to miss this wedding. God is good all the time, even though I did not get inside the church my attitude about it was good and I found an ideal spot right at the entrance. I saw everyone go in and I was able to see many faces I hadn't seen in years. I was glad to see them as they were glad to see me. It was a beautiful day and I was very comfortable under the huge shade tree at the entrance. I even had another dear friend come to the wedding and he chose to stand outside with me the entire time and we laughed and talked and greeted people. What I'm trying to say is negative things still happen in our lives but if you just be patient and keep a good attitude it could still turn around in your favor. I sent the nurse who was with me inside a few times to view the wedding and she took pictures. So even though I didn't get in the church I had a wonderful time just being there. Don't allow your attitude, your outlook or your view of life spoil your day. Look up and look around. God has created a beautiful day. Rejoice and be glad in it. My name is Jasper and these are my thoughts.

June 20, 2012

FATHER'S DAY AND THE QUAD

Father's Day brought such excitement to me I could hardly wait until it got here. My brother invited the family to have a BBQ at his house and I didn't want anything to stop me from getting there. It was a beautiful event. My brother was happy to see me as was my daughter and my grandchildren. It was an even more special event because my youngest daughter whom I don't see very often, 3 years as a matter a fact, was there. One point I tried to make is that don't let the wheelchair or your circumstance stop you from enjoying any part of life. Embrace each day as if it's father's day. Stay close to your family if you can, cherish your friends and keep a good attitude. I'll say it again, life doesn't stop just because your situation has changed. Live your life with all the gusto you can. Just a short note to encourage you to keep your chin up and keep pressing forward. These are my thoughts, my name is Jasper.

July 9, 2012

WE DO MATTER

Hello, my name is Jasper and I am a quad. Sometimes, in this condition we are in it may seem to us that life maybe passing us by whether you admit it or not. Sometimes, we may get feelings that say we don't matter, but we do! I found out a little more about how much I matter when I called a friend and she was very upset and distraught. You see she is now a widow and she is still grieving for her husband. I know she has all the skills and knowledge to cope with the problem, but we are human and sometimes we just get weak. I was so glad that I was able to talk to her and as well as I know her I was able to talk to her and ease some of her pain. The conversation I had with her I tried to be uplifting and encouraging and before we got off the phone she admitted she felt much better as she was glad that I called her. She said that my phone call really helped her through the day. So you see, even in our condition God puts us in a place where we can by most useful. That's why I say we do matter! We have the power still to ease someone's pain or to make someone's day. The power to make someone laugh or to forget about the situation that they are in. Yes, we do matter! My name is Jasper and these are my thoughts!

July 18, 2012

SPIRITUAL HOPE

Hello my name is Jasper and I'm a quad. I recently attended a church service in which they give prophecy over your life. They pray for you collectively as well as individually. They lay hands on you as being some transference of power. As for me the Pastor felt in his spirit if my faith is strong enough I will one day walk out of this chair. I've heard some really amazing things that people gave testimony to such as a woman walking after 35 years of not walking. I've heard testimony of someone literally dying during the church service and they prayed for her collectively and she started breathing. Now I don't know where you are spiritually or if you believe at all but I do believe that spiritual hope is a vital part of our recovery. Spiritual hope to me is like that gambler who believes in his heart that the next role of the dice is going to be a winner and if you lose that than you may as well pack up and go home. There have been all kinds of physical, mental and medical miracles in the world today. Tell me how can a man climb a mountain if he's blind. But it has been done. Or how can a kid survive under water for over 45 minutes and still live. Or someone being shot at point blank range and still live. These my friend are called miracles. Sometimes in spite what the Dr's may say, something will happen that the facts say should not have. There in lies my hope. I believe in a loving and caring God and if it be his will and if I do my part, I will stand up and walk out of this wheelchair one day. My name is Jasper and these are my thoughts.

July 25, 2012

ROUGH MORNING FOR THE SCI

My name is Jasper and I'm a quad. I have a C4 Spinal Cord Injury and as any SCI therapist will tell you every SCI is different. Lately, my blood pressure has been like a roller coaster - up today and down today. This morning my sinus' have been going wild. Every morning or every day may not be the same for an SCI. But still I like to bare in mind that my injury could be worse. So as best as I can I try to make my way through it. This is again the attitude we must have in order to recover. We can't afford to throw ourselves a pity party. That will only make you feel worse. Keep moving forward as best we can until things get better. This is what we must do every day. Sometimes I just get bored. I have to find some way to amuse myself. I ride in my chair up and down the hall, I speak to people - everyone, I may crack a joke to ease my boredom. These are the things I do to make it through my day. I try to participate in every activity. I can remember when I didn't want to be bothered with an activity but then slowly I figured why not. Now I love to participate in what's going on around me.

August 1, 2012

WHAT TO DO WHEN NEGATIVITY SETS IN

Hello My name is Jasper and I'm a quad and just like anyone else we all have good days and bad days. You ever have one of those mornings when you just didn't want to get out of bed and it's hard to get motivated and you feel like you're already running out of steam? Well, imagine how that would be along with not being able to move and do for yourself. I find that when I'm in that state of mind that's all it is - a state of mind. It means I have to smile maybe a little longer, crack a joke or two, hold my head up and keep going! As I've said many times, being a quad we can not afford to throw pity parties for ourselves. We must always strive to press forward no matter what the obstacle is. This can be done by getting involved and being concerned about someone else instead of yourself. It's hard to think of yourself when you're giving yourself away to someone else. This will help to bring you out of that negative state of mind. Everyday is not the same for normal people so I know it's not going to be the same for me. It's just something I have to learn to deal with and it's called life. My name is Jasper and these are a few of my thoughts.

August 22, 2012

MARRIAGE AND THE QUAD

Hello, my name is Jasper and I am a quad. I have been married twice in my life. My first marriage lasted 22 years. So, I feel as though I know something about the matter. But, I have never been married while being in a wheel chair. I was wondering to myself, what would that be like. I am sure all of the love, patience and all the other emotions are involved. But, still I wonder what it would like. It has to be something different. I would imagine it would take sometime for me to get over the feeling of being inadequate. For a man not being able to physically do things for his spouse. It weighs heavy on his mind. I believe as men, we are sort of trained as toddlers to be caring and nurturing towards our female counterparts. When you are in a position where you can't physically touch your spouse or being able to protect her if need be somehow makes you feel a little less than a man. So first, I believe for me I would have to get past that hurdle first. Not being able to do physical things for your spouse is like when a woman looses all her hair or looses a breast to cancer. It may not make a difference to her husband, but it is something that she has to mentally get past. So, since this is something that I have never experienced for myself I would appreciate some feedback.

Thank you,
this is Jasper

September 4, 2012

NO LIMITS

Hello my name is Jasper and I'm a quad. I would like to express to you my feelings about limiting yourself. We must learn that there are no limits because we are quads. I recently went on a fishing trip and they had a pole especially for me that was a sip and puff. I've never seen this type of car, but I was told there is a car you can operate with sip and puff. There are no limits to what we can do with determination and the technology they have today. I recently went to a jazz festival in downtown Detroit. There were lots of people everywhere but I managed to guide through them in my wheelchair. I went to all the jazz stages, I went to see all the vendors and I had a wonderful time. I did not limit myself because there were hundreds of people there. I did not let the size of the crowd intimidate me. I also went to my brothers house for a BBQ the following day because of the Labor Day weekend. All my children and grandchildren came by and I had a beautiful day watching my kids play with each other. I did not limit myself because my brothers house is not wheelchair accessible. We had a beautiful time right in the garage so I strongly feel this is something we must recognize. Don't limit yourself because of an event or the size of the crowd or some place that may be difficult. We can overcome almost anything if we want to. My name is Jasper and these are my thoughts.

September 12, 2012

FAITH

"Now Faith is the substance of things hoped for, the evidence of things not seen" (Hebrews 11:1). That was the lesson that was taught at my weekly bible study. It started me to thinking about my situation because we all hope for something that we can't see. But this thing called faith sometimes is the only thing we have to hold onto. It's the thing that keeps us hoping and giving us the desire to continue on. We can't see the changes in our situation, or the healing that's taking place in our bodies, or the renewing of our minds, but nonetheless we have faith that it's there and it's happening. All we need do for this act of faith to work is to believe that it will and then be patient and allow it to happen. It won't happen overnight, that would be a miracle. But a faith walk will take some time. How much time? No one knows, but again we must have faith that it will happen. There have been many acts of faith that have been documented and told by many people. People walking after many years of not being able to, or someone seeing for the very first time, people suffering with a situation for years and then suddenly being relieved of that situation. There are times in our lives when all of us must exercise a certain measure of faith to get through a situation. Without faith, we have no hope. Without hope, the spirit dies. And when that happens, you're somewhat doomed. So hold on to your faith until the very end.

September 19, 2012

BE YOURSELF

Hello my name is Jasper and I'm a quad but still that does not stop me from being who I am. I don't know who you may have been before your accident. Sure the accident takes a lot out of us but in time it all comes back. I'm speaking about your personality, your humor, your spirit, your thirst for life and anything else you may have had going for you. Sometimes things seem as though they'll never be normal again but be positive, be yourself and in time the wounds will heal. I go places such as concerts, movies, I'm still waiting to go on a date....ha ha ha, but in time who knows, anything is possible. What I'm trying to say is life goes on and even though we were sidelined for a moment we're not out of the game yet. So...be positive in your life, count your blessings, be a blessing to someone else, talk to other people in your condition who needs a pull up. There are so many things that we can do even in our wheelchair state. So be positive, be blessed and above all be yourself. My name is Jasper, good bye.

September 26, 2012

THE FALL SEASON

Hello my name is Jasper and I'm a native of Detroit and although I may complain a little about the change in temperature deep down I do love the fall season. I just bundle up a bit more and I go out and I enjoy watching the leaves turn on the trees. You would think that by being a Detroit native I would be used to the change of the seasons but not so. I complain along with everyone else. But like I said deep down I do love the change in seasons even winter time has a special appeal. It's so beautiful to see the fresh falling snow cover trees and bushes. It's an awesome work of God as he paints a beautiful picture for us. Things for me are a bit different having to be in my wheelchair. I can't rustle through the leaves like I used to or go walking in certain areas admiring natures handiwork but still I get out and it's a blessing to be able to see the seasons change. I don't know where you may live, if you have one season or you don't have the natural growth that Michigan has but I do love it. Good bye my name is Jasper.

October 24, 2012

IT'S ABOUT WHAT YOU BELIEVE

Hello my name is Jasper. I'm a quad. For the past couple of months I've been attending a church service where they promote self healing through spiritual beliefs. These beliefs come directly from the bible and you can actually heal yourself, someone else, cast out demons and overall enrich your life if you believe these things. The gentleman who teaches the class is known as an apostle lee. he prophesied over me and said that I would hear from the Lord and I can actually speak healing into physical existence. I was told that these things have actually taken place in church and I have to admit I have been there on occasions and saw people healed right before my eyes. I choose to believe that everything in the bible is true. And God is a God that cannot lie. And if he said he's taken all sins and diseases and paralysis and all sickness, He bore all our sicknesses on the cross. And it is said by my stripes ye are healed. I choose to believe that I'm exercising what I was told to do to call those things that are not as though they were. I don't know when the Lord will heal me but if I act according to His word I believe one day I will walk again. So hold on to your dreams and your faith, appease God and he may work a miracle in your life. This is Jasper and these are my thoughts.

November 1, 2012

THE HALLOWEEN PARTY

Hello my name is Jasper and although I'm in a wheelchair I still have fun. The facility where I live gave a Halloween party and to my surprise it was a lot of fun. Some of the workers dressed up in costumes and it was fun to watch them act a little crazy. They also had Karaoke, snacks and a costume contest. I really enjoyed the party and being around the people I live with. We all had fun. Wish we could do it more often. My name is Jasper and have a blessed day.

November 15, 2012

THE MOTOWN MUSEUM

Hello, my name is Jasper and I'm a native Detroiter who has never been to the Motown Museum. After I began to think about that I felt a bit ashamed that after all these years I had never visited there. It is truly a Detroit landmark loaded with tons of Detroit history. As I walked up to the building on West Grand Blvd and I stepped inside, the history began to engulf me. The tour guides were excellent as they began to describe how the Motown sound began. They told us about the Gordy family, their holdings, properties they owned, they explained how Berry Gordy borrowed $800.00 from his family and with the idea in his head and the $800.00 Motown began. It was amazing when the tour guides explained how one star who were then just kids lived right down the street from one another. When one kid entered Motown he went back and told a friend and eventually Motown had a stable of singers and performers all under 21 years of age. Right there on West Grand Blvd they were taught how to walk, talk, dress, and act a certain way because the lady who groomed them always told them they would be destined for greatness. They told us how Motown would take one song and remake it over and over, selling millions of records all over the world. Berry Gordy was a perfectionist in his craft. Sometimes he would polish a song for a year or two before he felt it was ready to be released. The sound studio was very simple. I walked in expecting to see a lot of fancy equipment but there was none. They were very inventive in the way they did things back then. Although, they did have a Steinway grand piano, the Steinway piano eventually wore out and it so happened that Sir Paul McCartney visited Motown Museum and had it rebuilt. I could go on and on about my feelings being in the Motown Museum and feeling all that rich history but here's what you should do...if you are a native Detroiter or a maybe not you should swing by the Motown Museum on West Grand Blvd to see where it all started. My name is Jasper and enjoy the trip.

November 21, 2012

THANKSGIVING

Hello, my name is Jasper and Thanksgiving for me is a time of reflection. I think back on previous Thanksgivings when we were all joined together as a family. Of course there's the food and the children, and that's something to be thankful for. Thanksgiving to me is a time when you should look back on your life and be thankful for where you are, and then pass on those feelings to someone else. The holiday says "Thanks" - thanks for all that the Lord has given you, all that he's given us, and the second part is the giving. Sharing of yourself- share your joy, share your life with someone else by giving. This holiday is truly much more than just a family meal. It's a time of love and giving that love to family and friends. Sharing and caring is what this holiday is all about.

December 19, 2012

IT'S ALMOST CHRISTMAS

Hello, my name is Jasper and although I'm a quad I still look forward to Christmas. Not in the same way I did as a child but I'm especially looking forward to being with family. My condition has made me much more affectionate toward family. Watching my daughters go through Christmas with their kids really gives me a zing. Watching my daughter prepare Christmas dinner, watching the grand kids run through the house full of joy really gladdens my heart. Just because you may be in a wheelchair or lost a limb or whatever your condition may be should not damper your spirit about the day Christ was born. I can hardly wait to be surrounded with all the love that I know is coming. It is also the time to reflect on past events of your life and knowing how blessed you truly are. I for one never overlook this point because I nearly lost my life twice. I know how blessed I am to still be here, to be able to share with family and friends, to be able to interact with the people around me. This is a season you should have nothing to be saddened about. The evil deeds in the world are diminished by the outward love people express at this time of the year. So I say do you join in, forget past differences, love on someone, family or not, and just be thankful for where you are right now. My name is Jasper, have a blessed holiday.

2013

January 3, 2013

HAPPY NEW YEAR

Hello my name is Jasper and another year has come and gone. I can hardly believe it's 2013. A chance for a new beginning, a fresh start. Old things are put away and we look forward to what's ahead. Each year I look at the new year as a new beginning. All my mistakes, regrets and whatever are forgotten and I feel refreshed and brand new. I want to make new plans for myself and watch it materialize within the new year. I stop worrying about what I didn't do or what I should have done and focus on promising things of the future. This is going into my fourth year as a quad and except for the obvious nothing has changed for me. I have the same desires and feelings, same motivation I had before the accident. Every new year just brings all that alive for me. So I urge you, whoever you may be, don't worry about the year past, but rather take this opportunity to focus on what lies ahead. Your faith, good or bad, all depends on you. Your attitude determines your altitude. Happy New Year.

January 18, 2013

LET'S GO BOWLING

Hello my name is Jasper and I'm a quad. Like a lot of people who are in wheelchairs it was difficult for me to adjust. Sometimes I felt as if my life had come to a standstill. I didn't know what to do or how to relate to other people in similar conditions, but slowly with the help of the staff at my care center I began to realize that life goes on. Just a few days ago I went on an outing to a bowling alley. Before I became a quad myself I never even thought of handicapped people doing something like bowling, but when it was suggested to me I decided to give it a try. I found out that there are a lot of handicapped people who bowl, and also it was a lot of fun! I got a lot of support and motivation from the staff and they even brought a special ramp for me and my ball. Oh! Did I fail to mention that I have gotten the highest score TWICE since I've been bowling? Well, not bragging but to make a point- if you feel down about your life because it has changed so much, rethink your attitude because life goes on. You have a choice- you can either sit by and watch it go by, or you can join in the fun and live your life as before. I go to movies, I've been fishing, I've been to the Opera, I go to concerts- my point is get off the pity pot and live your life. My name is Jasper- let's go bowling.

February 5, 2013

THINK POSITIVE

Hello my name is Jasper and I am a quad.

I've written a number of blogs and in all my blogs I try to create a positive image. It is said "as a man thinks", so is he so if we think positive we will be more likely to do positive. I try to find something positive or humorous in everything I do. As I ride through the hallways in my recovery center I speak to everyone I can, try to remember each person by name, and always greet them with an uplifting attitude. This is just a small thing but it has a lot of meaning, not only for me but also for the people I speak to. We no longer can do a lot of the things we used to so we have to think of new ways to fill our days. It can be by participating in things we have never done before. I never used to play BINGO a lot because I consider it to be an "old folks" game, but that's one of the activities that are offered here. At first I wouldn't play but with some encouraging from the staff, I began to play and now it is one of the activities that I most look forward to. I also try to join in whatever is going on at the center- it helps to not only fill my day but gives some meaning to my new life. So my message is stay uplifted, don't be afraid to change, try new things, and above all stay positive.

My name is Jasper, good-bye.

February 12, 2013

KEEP YOUR CHIN UP

Hello my name is Jasper and I am a quad.

I have been a quad since April of 2009 and although I live in a very nice recovery center, adjustment hasn't been easy. I try to stay positive- I smile a lot, I talk with other clients. I know just about everyone by name, yet sometimes my situation still gets the better of me. As best I can I try to follow the routine that's laid out for me. I have even been told by a Pastor that I would hear from God one day and he would tell me to get up and walk. I've had more than one person tell me they've been in my condition and now they're up and walking. Still sometimes it's a bit much for me to bear. So many complications to get past. Lately I've been having a lot of anxiety coupled with a touch of pneumonia. I try to smile and be positive and tell myself one day it will pass. I am saying all of this because you may be going through something as a result of your injury, but holdfast, be strong as possible, and above all be positive. Even though we have setbacks God spared us, that means we have some more living to do. Children that need us, parents need us, friends who love us, and at all times remember God knows best! Keep your chin up and continue on.

My name is Jasper and I am a quad. Good-bye

March 29, 2013

WORDS OF ENCOURAGEMENT!!

Hello my name is Jasper and I am a quad.

Sometimes when I sit and reflect on my life I can't help but feel a great sense of thankfulness. I owe all my thanks and gratitude to the Lord. Some of you may not believe but I know had it not been for him showing me grace and mercy I would not be here. There was a time in my life when I was crippled as a child, I've been through an addiction to drugs, I survived two car crashes, one which took the life of my wife, and I am still here. I don't worry about a lot of things today because just as Jesus said, these are meaningless and they will pass away anyway. The most important thing that we should be concerned about in our lives is preparing for your spiritual life. Make no doubt about it God is still running things, I have no control over anything. I must look to him for everything. The air I breathe, every time I swallow, my thoughts, waking up in the morning is all due to his grace. So I don't fret over what people think of me or financial matters, because I know that he will work it out for me in the end. So I encourage you that no matter what you may be going through, no matter how hard it is, look to the Lord and he will surely make a way for you. Easter is coming up soon and we should all focus on what Easter is really about. He died for us, he paid the ultimate price so that we may have a right to life. So that we will one day life with him in his kingdom. He loved us that much and that's something we should never forget or take lightly.

Again my name is Jasper and these are my thoughts.

April 16, 2013

DON'T SIT, RISE UP!

Hello my name is Jasper.

There comes a time in everyone's life when we are challenged by certain events. It may be an auto accident or the death of a loved one, or you may be fired from a job, maybe going through a divorce- all of which are life changing events. Even though sometimes we may be knocked off our feet by an event I say that's not the time to sit, that's the time we must rise up and meet the challenge. We've all had the wind knocked out of us at some time or another, but staying down or throwing a pity party or sticking your head in the stand will avail you nothing. It is this time we must rely on God above to pull us through and we rise up and find answers to our problems. If we just believe that God will help us we feel better, we feel encouraged, we find new strength, we also find doors will start to open when we apply ourselves. There have been lots of people that have gone through life changing experiences and learn to overcome. I remember reading about a blind man who was a mountain climber. A girl who had her arm bitten off by a shark yet she still surfs. Christopher Reeves who became a quad did not stop his life because of his circumstances; he became an advocate and helped change the lives of many. You see with God as your guide you have an unlimited source of strength and power. All you have to do is rise up and tap into that power. You will find that you can go further than you ever expected. The enemy only wants to blind you and confuse you by bad events that happen in you life, but God will take those very events to groom you and make you stronger. So I say don't sit, and focus on your circumstance, but rather RISE UP and tap into the source and move on.

Thank you my name is Jasper.

May 1, 2013

DON'T FALL INTO THE TRAP

Hello my name is Jasper and like most of us I have issues in my life. Little things that just pop up that annoy us. But don't let the little things in life distract you from what you should be focusing on. You may own a business or desire to own a business, you may already be in some school, or raising a family. These things require all of our focus if you are to succeed. Don't let little things such as someone telling you you "can't do it", doors that are closed in your face, setbacks and failures. Don't let these things stop you from your goal, these are just traps set up by the enemy to throw you off. God wants only the best for us, he points us in the right direction and he has a gift or a blessing at the end of our labor. But the enemy throws obstacles in our way to throw us off track. People that don't like me, people that hurt my feelings, feelings of inadequacy, feelings of failure thinking that certain things are for other people and not you. These are things that come to our mind because that's where the enemy attacks us. We must look past this and understand that if we give it our best, the Lord will do the rest. He only wants success and joy and happiness in our lives. We must come to a point where we understand this and that will increase your desire to press forward. It's good to know that the Lord has our back and that He will always be with us to help us, to guide us, if we allow Him to. He said in his word that "If I be for you, who then can be against you?" This should be a great comfort and support to you in life. You can do whatever you desire to do, because He will give you the strength to succeed. "I can do all things through Christ Jesus, who strengthens me". Believe it.

May 28, 2013

LET GOD TAKE CONTROL

Hello my name is Jasper and I'm a quad. I live in a rehabilitation center so I often see crippled bodies, people who are much worse off than I am. Some cannot move at all, some cannot speak, and some have emotional issues. But I say to you today, that the Lord is still in control. We must learn to look to him for our strength and the desire to go on. I don't know why he hasn't healed me or some others, but I still believe that he can and he will in his time as he sees fit. I'm thankful just to be alive because I know had it not been for the Lord I would be dead. I survived a life of drug addiction, and two near fatal car crashes, and I know in my heart that it was the Lord who saved me. I don't worry very much, I don't worry pretty much at all. Why should I be disturbed over things I can't control? Instead I just praise the Lord for what I do have. I can think, I can talk, I've been blessed with a wheelchair so I can move around, go places, and interact with people. I'm still blessed. So when you feel down and out, just remember you don't have to worry because the Lord who loves you is in control. If you talk to him, He will answer you and He will take care of any situation you may be in. You have to believe that.

My name is Jasper, love you, goodbye.

June 12, 2013

I CAN'T TALK ENOUGH ABOUT GOD

Hello my name is Jasper and I'm a quad.

I have no feelings in the lower part of my body at all. This may seem as quite an issue to some, but it doesn't worry me as much as I thought it would for I know and I believe that God is still in control of my life. Sometimes we all get thoughts that are not quite positive- I noticed that lately I've been getting thoughts that are not quite in line with what God wants. Thoughts of what I used to do in the past. I've been a quad for going on 5 years now- I haven't been able to even touch a female for those 5 years. I can't play with my grandchildren the way I used to. In short there are just a lot of things I love to do but can't do anymore. That gives the enemy an avenue in which to attack me through my thoughts. When I find myself thinking of relationships with females, I know it's the enemy that's taunting me. Then that's when I remember that the Lord says, fornication is a sin in the eyes of God. This helps to keep my mind, my thoughts, on the right path. Thinking of things I cannot do anymore is another way the enemy attacks me but again I say God can do anything that he wills for my life. He can turn a situation completely around if he desires. I don't worry about a lot of things. The thoughts that come are not only from Heaven, but are also thoughts from the enemy. I learned to separate and understand the two. Even though I'm physically challenged I still know that I am a blessed man. I still know that I have favor with God because of what he does for me each and every day. First of all I wake up at his will, I have the blessing of being in my right mind, I can breath, I have my eye sight, my hearing, and although I don't have much movement I still can turn my head. I can move my upper body and that is a lot more than what some quads can do, and I thank the Lord for that. He starts me on my day. I have many people that I associate with and a lot of people that know me. I have friends, good friends that I have been with for some 30-50 years, and that is a blessing. I have a wonderful family. I have healthy grandchildren that I am able to see and show love. All of that is God's will for me. I have only him to thank because I could have been dead, but he chose to let me live. So look at the bright points in your life when you are feeling negative. It's only a ploy by the enemy to upset your life. Focus not on your thoughts, but rather focus on God. Praise and worship him and your life will be fruitful.

Again, my name is Jasper and I am a quad. Thank you.

June 18, 2013

CLINICAL HEALING AND SPIRITUAL HEALING

Hello, My name is Jasper and I am a quad. Almost all of us will feel an ache or pain. We have certain conditions. We have concerns which lead us to go to the Doctor. He'll look us over and based on his clinical knowledge, he will make a judgement about our condition. He may even prescribe some therapy for us or write a prescription. Load us up on all sorts of medicines to help our condition. Often time they do work, but sometimes they don't. That's when we must look towards alternative medicines, natural medicines, that have been handed down through generations. We may even have to rely on a power much stronger than either of these. The Lord's word speaks of spiritual healing, to those who believe that Jesus walked this Earth, He healed the sick. He not only healed the sick, He cured the lame, He cleansed people of life long time diseases. He raised the dead. And these acts were witnessed by many people. Sometimes, even the Doctors, the Surgeons, can reach a point where they know they can go no further. They often won't admit it, but they look towards God for a miracle healing. As we all should know, your spirit is everything. When you're are on your sick bed, or you may be having problems in your life and you don't know where or who to turn to, if you lose your spirit, if your spirit is broken, you become weak and may not be able to make it through your situation. On the other hand, if you believe and have enough faith in the Lord, it will keep your spirit strong and vibrant. You will overcome things that some people may not understand. It is the spirit of the Lord that lives inside of us that can cure us, that can heal us, that can help us move forward, if you just have faith and believe. When Jesus left this Earth, He left instruction for us to live by. He told his disciples that I give you power to heal the sick, cure the lame. You may drink poision and it will not harm you, He even said that we would have the power even greater than He. To those who believe, Jesus said that we may ask anything of The Father in His name, and it shall be given unto us. If we believe this and our faith in the Lord is strong enough, you may lay your hands on the sick, near death person, and they may be revived. You may even lay hands on the cripple and they can walk again. You may be able to lay your hands on someone with a disease, in Jesus name, and they can be cured. These things are not in my imagination, these are actual events that have been witnessed. Think about this the next time you're going through a rough period in your life. Jesus said I will never leave you, nor forsake you. This should be a comforting thought, knowing that our Lord, our God, is there with us, always. And His word is true. Again, my name is Jasper and I'm a quad.

June 25, 2013

IT'S ALL ABOUT LOVE

Hello my name is Jasper and I am a quad. Most of my body is numb from my chest down. So, most things physically I dont feel. I cant do any of the things that I used to do or go to places I used to go. But occasionally I do get out and recently I went to hear my best friend preach a ceramon. He invited me to come hear him speak and I was so blessed to be able to make it. He spoke about love. The love of Jesus as he loved us. This started me to thinking about what the Lord required of us before he left this earth. It is quite simple, but for some of us is very difficult to do. He said, and I quote, "Love one another as I have loved you". This is all he wants of his people. That we should care, love, encourage, support, and help one another. If you have the love of Jesus inside you, if you allow his spirit to move you, loving another person should not be that difficult. Maybe some of us should take a self evaluation and see where your love meter reaches. What do you do when you see your brother in need of something? Or there may be someone you know that is hurting from a situation. What do you do when you know a child doesnt have a father and he needs male attention? What do you do for the widow, a woman who has lost her husband, and has no male presence in her life? Do you watch and ignore these things or do you help wherever you can? It doesnt always take money it can simply be a kind word every now and then, a phone conversation, a caring hug, or simply devote some of your time to a person who has no one. This is what I believe the Lord would want us to do. He does not want his people divided. He wants us to all be on one accord.

Loving and caring one to another. So, I encourage you to take a look at your life, how do you live it? Is it according to God's will? Or are you falling short? A lot of us claim to be children of God and yet we turn our backs for our brother in need. This is not God's way. Jesus said, "If your brother thrist, give him drink. If he hungers, feed him. If he is cold, give him your coat." How many of us have that type of thought in our minds and hearts? Very few I imagine. So think of these words the next time you have a opportunity to help someone. It's not about you or the person, but you are serving the Lord. Again, my name is Jasper and these are my thoughts.

July 3, 2013

FAMILY AND FRIENDS

Hello my name is Jasper and I am a quad. Just recently my best friend who happens to be a minister invited me to come and hear him preach. I was glad to hear from him and anytime I can I'm glad to go and hear him. He preached a very good sermon about the love of God. He comes from a very large family and coming up has a kid I pretty much grew up with him and his family. At the preaching event a lot of his family was there. Most of them haven't seen me in a long time because of my accident. I was the type of guy who liked to visit a lot so I saw them on a regular basis, but not so much anymore. As he spoke about the love of God, I began to think about how blessed I was to be there to see a lot of my old friends. We all used to run in the streets together. We used to party together, go to card games together, and cabaret together. This went on some 30-35 maybe 40 years ago. Just think we used to be in the world together, now we're all in the house of the Lord together. After all these years to be in the world then serve the Lord together a lot of people don't have that. You know when you get serious about serving the Lord, a lot of people shy away from you. You lose people, but I felt truly blessed that here were a lot of my friends serving the Lord with me. So think about this little story the next time you have an opportunity to be in church with an old friend or even a family member. It's truly a blessing from God to be able to think back where you were 20-30 years ago and see where you are now. God bless you and may God keep you and your loved ones. Again my name is Jasper.

July 3, 2013

YOUR COMFORT ZONE

Hello, my name is Jasper and I'm a quad in a rehab setting. We all have a comfort zone of some sort. It may be at a job, working at home, anywhere you've been doing something for a long time and you've gotten used to it. We are creatures of habit and sometimes it gets very hard to branch out and do something different. But, I believe that the Lord moves us according to His purpose. He knows just how to pull you away from your comfort zone. I believe he only does it to teach us and to elevate us to a higher level. Recently, I was called upon to do a workshop at the upcoming convention of Alcoholics Anonymous.
I have been very nervous about doing this workshop because I know I'll have to speak in front of a group of people. I am concerned about what I will say, I don't want to be boring, and I don't want it to be too short. But, I know deep down inside, the Lord just wants to pull me out of my comfort zone. Doing this talk will take me to a new level, it will only strengthen me with my people skills. So, I think the only thing I can do is pray about it and step up and do the best I can. I believe that the Lord would not ask me to do this unless He has me prepared. I won't worry about it. I'll just step up and do it. So, remember, if you are ever called upon to do something that may seem difficult for you, think of this, the Lord is just taking you out of your comfort zone to enhance you and to lift you up to a higher level.
Hello, my name is Jasper and these are my thoughts, be blessed.

July 16, 2013

THE GRACE OF GOD

Hello my name is Jasper and I'm a quad. With that being said as a quad we go through many emotional, as well as physical, changes in our lives. We often feel that our circumstances are unjust. We may even feel that God has done us a disservice. Some of us become so angry and bitter that it poisons us in relationships with other people. This may last for a period of time, but somewhere along the line we must remember that we are living on God's grace alone. I know for myself after being in two near fatal car crashes, going through a life of drugs, being a womanizer in the streets, sleeping with many women I did not know, and as a child surviving polio. All of which I realize today had it been not for God my life may have been much different. I could have been a cripple, I could have HIV or AIDS, I could have lost my life doing drugs, and I could have died in both those car crashes, but God's grace is sufficient and he allowed me to survive. We must understand that there are so many things that can ruin our lives, or even destroy us, but with God's grace we manage to make it through. Often times not even thinking it's Him, but of our own will. I see people everyday that their bodies are so disfigured or so paralyzed that they cannot move at all, or even speak at all. I know I am living on God's grace because I'm not one of those people. I can talk, I can think, I can communicate and express my concerns to other people, I can turn my head from left to right (which may seem like a small thing but I assure you if you could not do it it would become a big thing), and it's only because of the grace of God because in my last car crash I broke my neck in more than one place. So remember, the next time you may give yourself a pity party or you feel out of sorts because of things you can no longer do just remember- if you're able to wake up in the morning, know your name, and be able to count to ten, you're living on God's grace.

Thank you, my name is Jasper and I'm a quad.

July 25, 2013

VENGEANCE IS MINE.

Hello, my name is Jasper and I'm a quad. I would like to give some of my opinion and express my concern about the Trayvon Martin case. When I first heard about the case I was surprised that a person of color, or any person for that matter, can be murdered on the street and nothing is done about it. It only shows that our court system is flawed. It can work for you or it can work against you, depending on the powers that be. In this particular case you have a grown man armed with a gun who was told by police not to pursue the suspect, ignored the order, and as a result shot and killed an unarmed kid. This was not a man fighting for his life as he claimed, but a grown man fighting a kid. To me it doesn't matter what the race may be, this was a gross miscarriage of justice. I know that we're only human and we have emotions and feelings. When something of this nature happens to us, our first reaction may be to lash out, fight back, get vengeance. But I urge anyone reading this message that our Lord said "Vengeance is mine". He said do not hold malice in your heart for your fellow man. Pray for those who spitefully use you, forgive those who have done you wrong. The battle is not yours, and vengeance is mine. I know this may be a very difficult thing to understand but the Lord said "If ye are truly my disciple, you will heed my commands". There have been many people who have sought justice through not violence. Ghandi, Dr. King, and Malcom X, and as we all know the results were outstanding. If you are striving to live a Christian life you may be called to do a lot of things that are difficult to do, but remember the Lord said "to follow me you must first deny yourself". We don't have the luxury of doing everything we want to do, but rather follow his instructions because he is Lord. These are my thoughts, may the Lord bless you. My name is Jasper and I am a quad.

July 31, 2013

A PRAYER FOR DETROIT

Hello my name is Jasper and I'm a quad, also I'm a native of Detroit. I always enjoy growing up in Detroit. The 60s and 70s even the 80s was quit differnt it seems than today. There are so many things that have gone wrong with the management of Detroit that we've almost come to financial ruin. Along with that, people don't seem to cling together the way they used to. We have no outstanding leaders, no Coleman Youngs, no Ken Cockrels it seems that our city council can't agree on anything. I don't understand why so many of our leaders are so opposed to the city manager. We need help and if it has to come from an outside source, then so be it. If we could have handled the problem before we wouldn't be in this shape now. I believe we need someone to come in with an objective view of our situation and who has the guts to hire and fire whomever to straighten out the problem. The Kwame Kilpatrick administration did absolutely nothing to progress Detroit. Instead, he brought more negative controversy upon the city. Then there are the senseless murders that still go on in Detroit. The two men that were run down by a hit-and-run driver. There are so many kids being murdered in Detroit that you can lose count. I say all this about a city that I still love because Detroit needs prayer. As my mother often said "Prayer changes things." She would say that all the time and I knew in her heart she believed that. God said that his people have turned their backs on Him, but if they will just repent and obey his commands He would send healing throughout the land. Detroit I believe can still become a vibrant and exciting city to be in, but we have to do our part and come together as a city and we can't afford to leave God out. The churches need to stand up and be recognized. The church needs to be a voice within the city, standing on the Word of God and begin to minister and heal the land. We can no longer turn our heads away from things that are moraly wrong. We must begin to pool our resources together instead of the every man for himself mentality. I as well as my church hold a vigilant prayer for Detroit and we stand on the promise of God that He in His own time will heal our land. My name is Jasper and I'm a quad.

August 9, 2013

GIVE THANKS

Hello my name is Jasper and I'm a quad. At the Neurocenter where I live they have different activities to keep the clients entertained and stimulated. We do such things as go on outings (I just came back from an outing to Belle Isle). I've gone to baseball games, the Opera, concerts, and parties. This Sunday I am going to a church picnic and it's usually lots of people and lots of fun. Here at the facility where I live I just came in from viewing some antique cars. They were beautiful! All decked out in different colors- Corvettes, Charger, Cobra, Nova, and a '63 Chevy Impala. The point I'm trying to make is even though I'm confined to a wheelchair God still allows me to enjoy life just as anyone else does. It's a beautiful day today. I can go out, feel the sun on my face, feel the warm breeze in the air, smell the flowers, and just partake in this wonderful life that the Lord has given me. I take the advice that my pastor gives us and that is I don't look at my circumstance, I don't dwell on the negative, and I look at life as a gift from God. I call those things that are not as though they were. I choose to praise God and thank Him for just allowing me to be here. Sometimes we don't have to have something great happening in our lives to give praise to the Lord. Sometimes praise Him for just being here. Praise Him for the little things- being able to see your grandchildren, being able to see friends from your school, being able to be around good positive people. These are all blessings from the Lord. Think about it- everyone may not have what you have, so appreciate it and give thanks. May

God bless you and may God keep you. My name is Jasper and I'm a quad.

August 23, 2013

HE'S GOOD TO US

Hello, my name is Jasper and I'm a quad. Although right now I'm in a wheelchair, I know the Lord is still blessing me. Yesterday I went to a Tiger's baseball game. It was a beautiful day, I was with good friends, and I really enjoyed being part of the crowd. I liked watching people laugh, have fun, and enjoy themselves, especially the kids. They got a real kick out of the music that they play! This Sunday after church I'll be going to my high school reunion. Seeing old friends that I grew up with (we all went to school together) and after 40 or 50 years we're still friends. That in itself is a blessing from God. When He puts people in your life they are there for a reason. Sometimes they are there for only a season, then sometimes they stick with you through the years no matter what they watch you go through. Everyone does not have a blessing such as this. But I thank the Lord for having favor with me. I just go about my day and I appreciate the things the Lord has put in my life. Beautiful sunny days I can look upon, I'm always surrounded by good people that care about me. The Lord always gives people what they need. I'm in a wheelchair, I don't work, I don't have much money, but I live in a nice place, I'm fed every day, and I have clothes on my back. It's not my doing but it is my God's grace. So I encourage you to open your eyes and look around at the wonderful gifts that God has given you. Appreciate them. Goodbye, my name is Jasper.

September 3, 2013

STAYING ON TRACK

Hello my name is Jasper and I'm a quad. I also consider myself to live a Christian life. It is a life that I now believe was chosen not by me, but by God. Looking back at my past behavior I've always been the kind of man who was self-willed, stubborn, tunnel-visioned, seldom listening to what others thought about my actions. As a result I hurt people- my family, my mom, and my grandparents. But you know when people love you, I mean a for real love, they don't cast you aside that easily. God is no exception, He loves us whether we're good or bad. He wants us to always be obedient to His word but when we're disobedient to His word he loves us still. He loved me when I stayed out nights, He loved me when I drank, when I partied too much, when I lied, and when I threw temper tantrums. He loved me all through my addiction but I also believe that during your struggles He sends you messages through other people. He sends you signs that He's working in your life. Made people, especially my friends, talk to me and gave me sound doctrine. But you have to be willing to listen because the words that are coming from them, but they're speaking through the spirit of God. He's put these people in your life to keep you on track. If that doesn't work He will allow you to get in situations that you can't get out of. For instance, I was once stopped on the expressway by the police and I had things in my car that I should not have had. Suddenly they got a call and had to leave as something more important was happening, but that was God. I survived two near fatal car crashes- one in which I lost my wife. But still I did not listen to the messages He was sending me. I even had a woman tell me that the enemy was going to be after me and I should watch very carefully what I do and where I go. She said "the Lord has given you many blessings but he's going to get tired of you not living your life right, and you don't want the Lord to chastise you". I brushed off her warning thinking she didn't know what she was talking about, but sometime after I had my second car crash in April of '09. I realized the Lord had chastised me. I believe for being disobedient to His word because I had given my life to him in 1994 but I still hadn't stopped doing the things I was doing. Although he sent me many blessings I see where I ignored them all. I don't know if He got tired of me or not, but I do believe He decided to chastise his child. But believe it or not that doesn't bother me for the scripture says "He chastised those who He loved". He had no intention of letting me die out on the expressway but he did slow me down so that I could become the person He wanted me to be so I could reflect back on my life, see my mistakes, and work towards helping others. So I encourage you to stop and take a long look at your life, focus on the messages that God has sent you, ask yourself "what am I doing with my life? Am I being what God wanted me to be?" Don't wait until God has to stop you- you may not like it.

I'm Jasper, and be blessed.

September 25, 2013

WE ARE BLESSED

Hello my name is Jasper- Praise the Lord! I was watching the news and various other TV shows and as I watched the news I heard of so many killings, senseless murders, women and children being killed, 2 men shot one another in road rage, the chemical warfare and Syria, the flooding that they're having in Colorado, and the fires in California. So much killing and destruction going on today, but we who know Jesus and have the spirit of the Lord inside of us know that we are covered by his blood. I can't imagine today living my life outside of the body of Christ. But knowing Him, having a relationship with Him, I know I can call His name or say a prayer and ask Him to surround me with his angels or put a hedge of protection around me. And I believe with all my heart that he will hear my cry and protect me. This is a gift that a lot of people are sorry to say don't have. Like a lot of people even after I turned my life over to the care of God I did things that were not of God, but in time He opened my eyes by chastising me and it's a wonderful thing because scripture tells me "He only chastises those whom He loves". So I know to some it may seem like a horrible twist of fate but I understand why He allowed certain things to happen in my life. To calm me. To bring me into submission. To give me time to reflect on His word and to take a good look at the wonderful gift of life that He's given me. and I praise the Lord for that. So although we're living in a violent society filled with all kinds of traps and snares by the Devil, we do not fear because we know the Lord and his spirit, the kingdom, is inside of us. My name is Jasper, be blessed.

October 1, 2013

ALL ALONG THE WAY

Hello my name is Jasper, Praise the Lord! As I was sitting alone I began to reflect on some past events of my life when I was a child and had polio. I remember the doctors and my mother had me run down this long hallway. I remember the old man who asked me to get into his car. I remember my mother fighting with my stepfather. I remember my mother longing for a husband, a home, and a better life for us. I remember a lot of dangerous times during my drug addiction- my addiction with crack made me a totally different person than I am now. I thought about the events surrounding my two near fatal car crashes. As I reflected upon all these things that happened in my life, even today the institution where I live, I can clearly see where God brought me through it all. I wasn't supposed to walk but God said yes. He brought my mother through two bad marriages without being harmed. Many times I found myself in places I had no place being. I was out all hours of the night, going days without sleep, and doing much harm to my body. But the Lord still had favor with me, even though I was messed up He still showed me mercy and grace. I did not know that I was going to have a second near fatal car crash when I bought my insurance. I think it was no more than a couple weeks after I bought it I had the accident. The insurance I have pays for my housing where I live. I didn't know but the Lord knew I was going to need that insurance. All through my life I now see that the Lord has carried me, protected me, guided me, and loved me when I thought no one else did.

Everything I am, everything I have- my wonderful children, my grandchildren, and the mothers of my children- I owe it all to the grace of God. So I urge whoever is reading this when you feel that you can't go on, or that life has dealt you an awful situation, whatever it is God will take care of you just as He's taken care of me. He loves me and He also loves you. Hold on to your faith and just be patient. He is with you always, even till the end of time.

My name is Jasper, be blessed.

October 29, 2013

ALWAYS PRESS FORWARD

Hello my name is Jasper, Praise the Lord! As I was sitting alone I began to reflect on some past events of my life when I was a child and had polio. I remember the doctors and my mother had me run down this long hallway. I remember the old man who asked me to get into his car. I remember my mother fighting with my stepfather. I remember my mother longing for a husband, a home, and a better life for us. I remember a lot of dangerous times during my drug addiction- my addiction with crack made me a totally different person than I am now. I thought about the events surrounding my two near fatal car crashes. As I reflected upon all these things that happened in my life, even today the institution where I live, I can clearly see where God brought me through it all. I wasn't supposed to walk but God said yes. He brought my mother through two bad marriages without being harmed. Many times I found myself in places I had no place being. I was out all hours of the night, going days without sleep, and doing much harm to my body. But the Lord still had favor with me, even though I was messed up He still showed me mercy and grace. I did not know that I was going to have a second near fatal car crash when I bought my insurance. I think it was no more than a couple weeks after I bought it I had the accident. The insurance I have pays for my housing where I live. I didn't know but the Lord knew I was going to need that insurance. All through my life I now see that the Lord has carried me, protected me, guided me, and loved me when I thought no one else did.

Everything I am, everything I have- my wonderful children, my grandchildren, and the mothers of my children- I owe it all to the grace of God. So I urge whoever is reading this when you feel that you can't go on, or that life has dealt you an awful situation, whatever it is God will take care of you just as He's taken care of me. He loves me and He also loves you. Hold on to your faith and just be patient. He is with you always, even till the end of time.

My name is Jasper, be blessed.

November 5, 2013

WHO HAS YOUR BACK?

Hello my name is Jasper- Praise be to the Lord.

Do you remember a time in your life when you felt alone? Or maybe a time when you felt everyone was against you? Or even a time when you didn't know how you were going to make ends meet? But somehow you got through all of that and you were able to keep going. Do you ever remember a time when you put your trust in someone and they let you down? Do you ever remember running out of money and resources and had no one to turn to? But still you made it through these tough times. Have you ever been ill...I mean so ill you thought maybe you weren't going to make it? Or has the doctor ever told you that you had HIV or Cancer or something that knocked you off your feet? Somehow you found the strength and the spirit to keep going and you got past it. Well, I'm here to let you know it was no one but the Lord who had your back all the time. Sometimes we get in a situation that seems so hard to bear we forget who has our back. He said in his word He'll never leave you nor forsake you, saying that He will walk down every road with you, He will not forget about you, He will take care of you, even when you're not aware of it. So I want to say hold on to your faith, keep praying, and keep pressing forward because He's got your back.

God Bless, this is Jasper.

November 14, 2013

MIRACLES STILL HAPPEN

Hello my name is Jasper- praise the Lord! Some people don't believe that the Lord exists. There are some people who do not believe in divine intervention. But here are two stories that actually happened that may change your view.

I believe it happened in Colorado where there was a terrible flood. There was a lady in an SUV who was trapped by the flood waters, her SUV with the windows rolled up tightly slowly submerged and went under the water. Rescuers tried desperately to reach the SUV as it was submerging. One man happened to reach under the water and he felt her hand, and he was able to grab her and pull her to the surface. It was an ordeal but the woman was saved. When they brought the van up out of the water the windows were still closed tight, just as it was when the van went under. So my question is, how was he able to pull her out and the windows were still shut tight? I don't know about you but I believe that it was divine intervention and God performed a miracle.

I'd like to tell you about another story- there was a terrible accident and the rescuers were having a difficult time getting to the person inside. It was a woman and the car was an old Mercedes Benz, and it was very difficult to rescue her because the car was so strongly built. I suppose the woman assumed she was going to die, so she asked for prayer. No one saw where he came from but a priest suddenly appeared. He prayed for the woman, then he told the rescuers their equipment will work now. Then they rescued the woman, they looked for the priest to thank him, but nowhere could he be found. No one saw him come, and no one saw him leave. Even though there were some 70 photographs taken at the scene the priest was in none of them and they could not find him anywhere. So I ask you, what do you believe? Do you have an answer for what occurred? Or do you believe it was a miracle from God? I prefer the latter.

My name is Jasper, praise the Lord.

November 19, 2013

STRANGE AND PECULIAR PEOPLE

Hello my name is Jasper- Praise the Lord!

The world- and when I say the world I'm talking about those people who live by their own agendas. The people who don't believe there is a God. The people who speak against God. The Christian people that know God but seem to always go against His word. I'm talking about society at large. They believe that if someone hurts you, you almost have a responsibility to hurt them back. They're often selfish people thinking only of themselves, some of them never express love or understanding towards another person. They have their own idea of what is good and fun in their lives, some of them feel that they create their own circumstances in life. But there is a society of people who make up the church the way God intended them to. They live and are guided by the word of God, they don't do as the world does. When they are confronted with a situation they always remain calm. When people show hatred toward them they are quick to understand and forgive. They are quick to pray for that person and always show them kindness. They help people that they don't even know and are happy to do it. They don't practice the things that people in the world do. This society of people don't drink, they don't believe in body art or body piercings, they don't believe in any violent behavior, the only time they dance or shout or show any outward emotion is in praising their God. The world view these people as "different" and "strange". "Strange" because they don't act the way most people do. The reason for that is they live their lives according to God's word. They live a life of meekness and forgiving, keeping their bodies clean and holy as the Lord commanded. They live as it is said by Jesus himself "Man does not live by bread alone, but by every word that proceedeth from the mouth of God". The world looks at these people and their strange habits and they don't understand, how could anyone be that nice and understanding? That is because they don't know the word of God. This type of life is for anyone that wants it, but you must first come to the Lord- His arms are open and He waits for you. He says "I come to give you life and that more abundantly. Take my yolk upon you, for my yolk is light and easy" meaning if you live your life according to the word of Jesus you will surpass many obstacles. Your life will be smooth, calm, and easy. You will learn to love others as He has loved you. So I urge you to come to Jesus and you will then understand the "strange" and "peculiar" people.

My name is Jasper, and God bless.

November 22, 2013

REMEMBERING JFK

My name is Jasper, praise the Lord!

I was just a kid in Elementary school when all of a sudden teachers started running through the halls, they were crying, they were all upset, and I learned later that President Kennedy had been shot. I remember the whole nation, it seemed like every neighborhood, was upset and crying. He was truly a remarkable man coming from a remarkable family. It seemed that he was a President that truly cared about the people. He was always pushing the people to do better academically and even though he had severe back pain himself he promoted exercise programs for kids. He was one of the nation's best presidents in my opinion and we still think of him and miss him today.

My name is Jasper, be blessed.

November 26, 2013

IT'S THE HOLIDAY SEASON

Hello my name is Jasper, all glory to God.

Once again it's the holiday season. Thanksgiving is here, people are cooking, and families are planning to spend time together. There is so much talk about Christmas you almost feel as though Christmas is already here. People planning on what they're going to buy, so much talk about Black Friday and "Black Thursday", and so on and so forth. People are doing so much planning and rushing around preparing for Thanksgiving dinner, where they're going out of town, as I said people are already making plans for Christmas. As for Thanksgiving have you asked yourself "What am I truly thankful for?" Is it the gathering of my friends and family? Is it the fact I have a home that I can invite them to? Or am I thankful to God for all the blessings that He has provided for me? Do I realize that I don't have to be here, or I could be in a hospital, or in some other grave condition. Have I taken time to properly thank God to be able to be here to see this holiday? Have I made time for him in this holiday season? and as for Christmas- the world views Christmas as the biggest money making holiday of the year. As it gathers close to Christmas people are rushing about, often times spending money they don't have trying to please everyone they can. Sometimes trying to do more than they did last year. Their thoughts are full of commercials about Christmas, it's all about the gifts and making people happy.
Nothing wrong with doing nice things for your family at Christmas, but don't forget what Christmas should truly

be about. First of all it's the birth of our Lord and Savior- don't overlook that. He is the reason for this holiday season. Make time to spend time in prayer to the Lord- thanking Him for all that He's done for us. All He wants us to do is to love one another, protect one another, support one another with love. Offer yourself and your time to a charity to help those who are less fortunate. Take a chance, open your heart, and do something for someone you don't even know. I'm sure everyone knows someone that's going through a bad situation. They may have tragedy in their home, they may have a loved one that is near death, they may not have the money to give their children a Christmas. God says "if you have abundance it is your duty to help the less fortunate". What He's saying is don't just think about yourself at Christmas, love someone that you don't have to love, show them the same love that I showed you when you were still a sinner. This is what Christmas is truly about- helping someone who does not have what you have, doing it purely out of love for the other person.

My name is Jasper, Happy Holidays and praise the Lord.

December 3, 2013

WHAT IT'S ALL ABOUT

Hello my name is Jasper, praise the Lord!

Once again I want to encourage my fellow Saints, my brothers and sisters in Christ. We are not to celebrate the upcoming season for the same reasons that the world does. They believe it's all about pleasing one another with gifts and all sorts of merriment, but I encourage you to remember what Christmas is truly about and it's the Lord's birthday. We are to be reminded of that special day when He was born and how He went about the business of changing the world, teaching God's people, and dying for us while we were yet sinners. Nothing wrong with buying gifts, being happy about the season- but don't forget about God. Don't get wrapped up and lose focus on what it's really about, loving one another just as He loved us. Doing for those who do not have what you have. Helping those who don't have the means to make their families happy. Reaching down and pulling your brother or sister up at a time like this. This is what the Lord God said that we should do, like any good father He wants to see all his children loving, supporting, helping one another to be happy. So remember don't get caught up in worldly things, but rather focus on the Savior of the world.

Again my name is Jasper, and we praise the Lord.

December 12, 2013

WITH ME ALL THE WAY

Hello my name is Jasper, praise the Lord.

I turned 60 years old on December 11th, and even though I'm in a wheelchair I feel great. I'm 60, feel 40, act 30, and it's all a blessing from God. I know this because I know all the abuse I've put this body through and yet some people didn't want to believe I'm 60. I know in my heart it's the Lord's blessing to me because I couldn't help but think of my drug using years, the sleepless nights, the garbage I put in my body. I was truly abusing my temple. The hanging out for long hours, sometimes long walks to get dope, having sex, just living an unsafe life. Someone close to me even commented to my surprise "Jasper, I never thought we would even make it to 50". I often thought about that statement and I said to myself "really, am I that bad?" Apparently so. But I know today that God continued to bless me even through my sinful ways. He has always provided a lot of support for me through friends and family, He has always pointed me in the right direction, and medically they say I'm somewhat sound. I say to myself "how could this be, when they check me they find nothing wrong?" But I know all the stuff they put in my body. It has to be the Lord showing me favor. I'm glad to be 60- it feels good to watch my children have children, I have friends that have been with me over 50 years, I still have my senses and my well-being even though I'm in a wheelchair. I feel great! I feel blessed to have so many people wish me well on my birthday. It's not me, but the spirit of the Lord that lives inside me. So when you're alone sometime think of the blessings that He has given you throughout your life. Think of all those that have gone on before you and you're still here. Trust me- it's only because of God's good grace.

Again my name is Jasper, praise the Lord.

December 23, 2013

GOD SPEAKS THROUGH PEOPLE

Hello my name is Jasper, all praise to the Lord. The place where I live is a rehab facility and I had a resentment against one of the female workers. I spoke to her in the hallway and she gave me a cold shoulder so I approached her again to try to find out why, she totally ignored me when I tried to talk to her. That made me angry, she is much younger than me, the same age as some of my daughters. I felt disrespected and I said to myself if she won't talk to me I won't talk to her. As a matter of fact I won't speak to her anymore and I'll totally ignore her. The Holy Spirit that lives inside of us will give you a little nudge to let you know you are doing something wrong. We must learn to pay attention to that feeling you have because that's God giving you a heads up. I didn't speak to her one morning and I speak to everyone in the morning, but when I didn't speak to her it made me feel funny. I felt it was wrong. When I went to church that next Sunday, they preached about love. The Lord commanded us to love one another just as he loves us unconditionally. It doesn't matter what a person has done to you, we must forgive them just as Christ forgave us. This is what He commanded us to do and He also said "If you love me, you will follow my commandments." The sermon really touched me and I felt as if the Lord was telling me through His word that I was wrong and I must make it right. So when I got back to the rehab, I approached the young lady and told her I wanted to speak with her. She can back shortly and we went to my room and we talked. I told her I had a resentment against her and the Holy Spirit spoke to me and said I must get rid of it, I must correct my wrong and forgive otherwise I'm being a hypocrite to the Lord. Talking with her, she told me she knew what she had done and she was having an awful day. As a matter of fact what she was going through that day made her go to the lady's room and cry. I appologized to her and she appologized to me and I found out that she's a wonderful person. It was just an unclean spirit in me that told me she ignored me so I must ignore her, but this is not the way God said we should live. We have to always express love to those around us so that they may see the Jesus in us. We must always be aware that the enemy is always looking for a way to gain. Put on the whole armour of the Lord and be ready to deal with the enemy when he comes. I want to say to you never forget who you are and whose you are. Again my name is Jasper. Praise the Lord.

December 30, 2013

NEW YEAR'S RESOLUTION

Hello my name is Jasper, Praise the Lord!

Well soon it will be a new year. As the new year approaches I think of things of the previous year and I feel even more blessed to still be here. I wonder how many people think about what a blessing it is to be here, to see a new year. Every year you could hear people talk about New Year's resolutions- some vow to lose weight (that's a popular one), they vow to move up on their jobs, or they vow to get a new car, and they vow to reach other goals that are material. But how many people vow a resolution to get closer to God? Make a resolution to change your life on a more spiritual level. How many people vow that they are going to read the bible more often and to live God's word? How many people vow a resolution that they are going to love people more than they have before? The Lord said "Don't set your sights on material things, but rather look towards those things that are in Heaven". Make a vow to get in touch with the Jesus Spirit that lives inside of you. Make a vow to research the Lord Jesus and what He stood for. Those that believe that He is the Son of God, that He came to Earth wrapped in mortal flesh, did supernatural things such as raise the dead, heal the sick, made the blind see, and other wonderful things for people. How many believe that He took on our sins and all our sicknesses and, most importantly, He shed his blood for us, that we may have a right to everlasting life. He died so that we may have life and have it more abundantly. We did not deserve such an honor, but He did it out of love for us. Don't you think you should make a New Year's resolution to get to know more about a man like that? We live only because He died for us. I think people should vow to get closer to the Lord and you can only do that by reading his word. It's not about what family you came from, your race, what you believe in, it's not about your money or your social position, but it's about Him. Our lives exist only because of His love for us. Learn to love Him and you can only do that by learning His word, what it stands for, and vow to live it. That should be everyone's New Year's resolution. That's just my opinion.

Again my name is Jasper, and Glory to the Lord. Happy New Year!

2014

January 3, 2014

FINDING YOUR WAY

Hello my name is Jasper, glory to the Lord.

This blog is dedicated to the sons of a dear friend of mine. Her name is Jerri Lynn and her two sons are Zach and Jeremy, and like most of us they have problems. Some problems that we have in our life are easily seen with our natural eyes, some problems we cannot see. Some problems we have in our life are caused by unclean spirits. These unclean spirits are strong, powerful, and they're good at what they set out to do. They cloud our good judgement and make us do wrong things, and we may believe we're doing something right. The Lord who loves us is aware of these unclean spirits, and He sends us messages through people who love us. Like I said these unclean spirits cloud our judgement, so often times we don't take the advice of our loved ones. You may be having conflict with your relationships, you may have stress on your job, you may have struggles with substance abuse, you wonder why you keep going over your limits. These are all the results of an unclean spirit keeping you away from the good spirit of Jesus that lives inside us. You may not believe that what I'm saying is true, but the Bible speaks of these things and I believe everything in the Bible is true. The Bible is our guideline and our basis on which we should live our lives. Make a positive effort to live a relationship with the Lord, even if you don't believe just take a look at it. Learn what the Lord wants of you and cling to it and you will see your life will change. The closer you get to the Lord the more He will reveal things to you and you will begin to see life clearly. I pray for Jerri Lynn and her entire family whether they know it or not. They are a close and loving family- beautiful sons and daughter. Don't let the enemy creep into your family circle and keep you divided. The Lord said "First seek the Kingdom of God and He will direct your path".

My name is Jasper, I love you all and praise God.

January 7, 2014

IT'S STILL A BEAUTIFUL WORLD

Hello my name is Jasper, all praise to the Lord!

I live in a rehabilitation center. I live my life in a wheelchair, and so do many other people here. Everyday I see wheelchairs, crushed bodies, people who can't talk, can't move, some with severe head injuries. But I've learned not to look at a person's circumstances, not even my own, and I focus on the love of God. As I look out of my window everything is covered with snow, yet somehow it's all very beautiful. The snow covered trees, all the ground is white, rooftops are white with snow- it's as if the Lord has painted a beautiful picture for us to see. There's nothing more beautiful than to look out your window or as you're driving along- the scenery is like a postcard. Some people complain about the snow and the cold weather but think about this- just as the Lord gives us beauty and nature in the Spring, Summer, and Fall, He also gives us beauty in the Winter. Also at the same time the cold air kills germs. It's good for us to breathe in the crisp, cold air. It cleanses our lungs, tightens our pores, the overall Winter climate is good for us. God knows exactly what He's doing, after all He's the one who created Earth just for us. Don't complain about the snow and cold weather but rather embrace it, think positive, and enjoy it. The Lord has us in His care and if the cold weather was not good for us He would not have it here.

Again my name is Jasper, all praise to the Lord.

January 23, 2014

REMEMBERING MLK

Hello my name is Jasper, Jesus is Lord.

A few days ago we celebrated the birth of Martin Luther King. I'm old enough and blessed enough to have lived during the last years of Dr. King's life. During Dr. King's birthday celebration across the nation, my mind drifted back to things I remember about him. I could remember my family taking me along to downtown Detroit (Cobo Hall) to hear Dr. King deliver a speech. There were lots of people there and I remember it because it was the first time I saw The Temptations in person. They were entertaining the crowd, and like many others I suppose also lending their support. I remember being in Junior High School when Dr. King was shot. There was a lot of social unrest, and the older kids from High School came by our school and they were angry and throwing rocks through the windows. We were scared in our classrooms and were confused about what to do. I'm not sure I remember the trip home, but I believe my mother probably picked me up like she often did. I can remember the National Guard and the policemen walking patrols down our street, I can remember seeing tanks and armored vehicles going down our streets. The news on TV was just filled with violence all over the nation. They spoke of killings, brutal beatings, snipers, and it was a scary time. I can remember seeing troops camped at Central High School, which was one of the headquarters. They had so many tanks and trucks and soldiers on the school grounds, but think of the irony. There was so much violence and social unrest, but Dr. King stood and died for his belief in non-violence. I'm sure that if he had anything to say about it he would not have wanted people to act this way. I'm sure he did not want his death to be a reason to go out and commit violence. I remember Dr. King in my mind and in my heart as a true man of God. He kept God's commandments and no matter how rough the times got he did not defer from God's word. He remained peaceful, kind, forgiving, and loving til the very end. He is a true example for all of us, just as Jesus was in His day.

My name is Jasper, praise the Lord.

January 29, 2014

WHAT WILL THEY THINK?

Hello my name is Jasper, praise the Lord.

Some people often make the statement "I don't care what the next person thinks of me". They may say "it doesn't matter what people think of me when I'm dead and gone". But I feel that it does matter what people think of you. I was one who used to boldly say "I don't care what people think, I'm going to do what I want to do regardless", but as I've gotten older I began to realize it matters a great deal what people think of you. It's a good feeling when you can enter into a room and everyone is glad to see you, or when people go out of their way to do something special for you. It should make you feel good when a friend, or even a stranger, does something for you that they don't have to do but they do it out of love and concern for you. You cannot get people to feel that way about you unless you carry yourself in a certain way. We all have moments where we are short tempered or we get irritated about something. We all have moments where we may say or do something we later on regret. But we all are just human and we make mistakes, but we learn from them. We learn to apologize for our shortcomings and we move on. When I leave this world I would like to think that when people think of me they will think of good times- they will think of things I did to try to help them or someone have a better day. Having the word of God within me helps to keep me calm, gives me peace, and causes me to express love and concern for others. No I'm not perfect, no one is. But when you give your life to the Lord, when people see you they should also see Him. I'm often concerned about what people think of me because they should see first the spirit of Christ that lives within me. When you live a Christ-like lifestyle things change for you. People feel good when they're around you, the Christ in you spills over onto them. Sometimes you ask yourself "what will people think of me when I leave this world?" Will some be glad that you're gone? Will some reflect on the fond memories of you? When I leave this world I hope that I leave a happy impression on people. When they think of me they will smile and remember that I tried to help them along the way. I tried to be a positive element in their life. I would like to think that they often saw the Christ in me, and not the real Jasper. So I urge you to take time and reflect on this. When I'm dead and gone, what will they think?

My name is Jasper, love and peace be with you.

February 3, 2014

EMPOWERMENT

Empowerment- to give <u>power</u> or authority to; authorize , especially by legal or official means.
To enable or permit.

Hello my name is Jasper, praise the Lord.

The dictionary gives this definition of empowerment. It is to give one authority and power to complete a task or to go further in one's life. Empowerment also means to elevate yourself to a higher level, always pressing forward to a higher goal. This is why the Lord left us with the Holy Spirit- to give us power, strength, and encouragement. He left this portion of himself in each of us so that we may be able to complete any task that He calls us to do. Some people may become afraid or fearful of what lies ahead for them, but the Lord did not give us spirit of fear, but one of encouragement. And through faith in Him we are always empowered to move forward. Empowerment means authority- always remember we have authority over our lives. Authority also means something of great importance. When you are empowered you have no such thing as "low self-esteem" or a "self-defeating attitude". Empowerment means holding your head up high, chest out, taking long strides towards your goal with confidence.
Empowerment gives you capable means of doing whatever it is you desire to do in life. You have complete permission by the Lord, through his empowerment to you, to have anything you desire.

Empowerment permits you to be anything, do anything, complete any task which lies before you. There is a scripture that says "I can do all things through Christ Jesus who strengthens me". That scripture speaks of empowerment through Christ Jesus to accomplish any goal you may desire. Any time you feel weak or feel that your life is somewhat in a rut, remember that scripture and remember that you are empowered by the most high authority. You have divine empowerment given to you through grace of our divine Lord. So with that in mind, why would one even consider the thought that you cannot do or complete whatever you want? It's just not so. Check your faith and remember- all things are possible to him who believes because we are empowered through Christ.

Hello again, my name is Jasper, and I am empowered.

February 18, 2014

FRIENDSHIP

Hello my name is Jasper, I praise the Lord.

I would like to speak on the subject of friendship. Friendship is something that's very important to me. It's important how I relate to people, especially my friends. I have been blessed through the grace of God to have friends that have been with me for some 30 to over 50 years. Some of my friends we've had the pleasure of sharing our lives together from elementary school to being in our sixties. We partied together, we grew up together, we ran the streets together, we watched as our first babies were born, we watched as our families grew, and now our babies are having babies. This is something that I don't take lightly and I praise God for the people that He put in my life. I don't believe it was anything that I did that was so special or that I was so great that I attracted these people, but I know today that everything that has happened in my life is by God's grace and glory. I know this because I have met people who don't have any friends. I have met people who can't seem to keep a friend for more than a few months. I've also met people that have been betrayed by friends or had friends who turned their backs on them. So I think about this sometimes and I thank God for the people that He put in my life who stuck by me when I was at my lowest point. Who is always there to lend a hand to me when I needed help. Jesus said the Father will always give you what you need and I know that He will also give you the people that you need. I consider my longtime friends to be gifts from God, to help me through the hard times in life, to share in my joy, and also to help comfort me in my pain. I recall once I was in a rehab and I was at a low point in my thinking, and I mentioned to one of my friends that I felt like giving up. The very next day two of my friends came to talk to me, to help pull me up, and told me that giving up on myself was not an option. I thank God again for the people He put in my life. I've had my friends take me into their homes when I had nowhere to lay my head. God knew what He was doing when He put these people in my life. So if you have a friend that has stuck by you, tell that friend how much you love them and appreciate them for being in your life. Remember, it's not you who attracts these kind of people, but it is God giving you more of what you need.

Goodbye, my name is Jasper. Praise God.

March 3, 2014

WHERE DO YOU STAND?

Hello my name is Jasper, praise the Lord.

I pray that my words today don't offend anyone, but I feel that the church is so divided because a lot of Christians refuse to stand up for the Lord's word. I was in a group session recently as someone was reading the current news of the day. There was an article in the news about homosexuality being widely accepted by the younger generation. I presented a comment to the reader and her reply was "that's a very sensitive and touchy subject" and I replied "well that's the kind I prefer to talk about". The point I'm trying to make is whenever we hear or see something that we know is contrary to God's word, we should be about the business of standing up for God. We do not have to argue about His word, but merely correct what we know is wrong and stand on His word no matter what. It should come as no surprise to the Christian when we hear or see certain things happening in the world today. We know that the Lord predicted all of these things many years ago. He said that before He comes back men will turn their backs against God. They won't heed God's word, but they will choose to go their own way, use their own devices, be lovers of themselves, their hearts will be waxed cold without regard for their brother. That's why it seems that anything goes in the world today. Kids killing parents, sexuality, and vile behavior is actually glorified. As I watch the television there are many new shows about zombies, "Walking Dead", eating people, new shows about vampires, new shows about witchcraft. And these things are being piped into our minds. These are not shows that our children and young people should be watching- they do have an effect on certain people believe it or not. I recently was talking to a young lady who watched one of these shows and she said afterwards she couldn't sleep for a few days. Make no mistake about it, we are always in a spiritual warfare and the only weapon we have is the word of God. As we look around at the world today things have drastically changed from the way they used to be- and it's not for the better. The world seems to be moving further and further away from God. They're trying to erase God from everything- the schools, the courtrooms, even the very government is trying to erase God out of the system. We need to be willing to stand up for God at every turn. It has to start at the family level and extend to every facet of our lives. Remember Paul said "we war not against flesh and blood, but the principalities of darkness". We war against things that we cannot see. Some people- even Christians- don't believe, but if you read God's word it will open your eyes and you will see. So I encourage you to be steadfast in the word, keep the faith, and press forward.

My name is Jasper, praise the Lord.

March 6, 2014

WHAT ABOUT TODD?

Hello my name is Jasper, praise the Lord. Many people have said that God works in mysterious ways, well I don't think so. If we read the scriptures He is very definite in what He wants us to do and what He does NOT want us to do. He is not wishy-washy but He is rather straightforward. I would like to dedicate this blog to a friend of mine named Todd. Like most of us I imagine Todd had goals and desires for his life. He probably envisioned his life going a certain way. But Todd ended up in a wheelchair for some 20 or more years. In those 20 years in his wheelchair he faced many obstacles. He quickly learned that the world makes it very difficult for people in wheelchairs. So he began to learn how to get around these obstacles, he learned a lot about insurance companies, people that are in the medical field only for the money. But Todd truly cares about people who have met with unfortunate circumstances and he makes it his business to help people who cannot help themselves. He lets us know when new devices come on the market, he introduces us to people who have learned to live a fruitful life being a quad. Being a quad does not mean that your life is over. It does not mean that you have to stop doing what you love, but rather find ways to do it differently. Sometimes we feel our lives should go the way we planned them, but then fate steps in and everything is turned upside down. It may be an auto accident, it could be the death of a loved one, it could be a divorce, or perhaps a financial disaster. But whatever it is it turns our world completely around. We don't understand it at the beginning but later on when we look back we can see how God put us on a different course. If Todd had not been a quad in a wheelchair he would not be as passionate about helping the wheelchair community. But God changed his life (and also his heart) and made helping seemingly helpless people live a better life. I thank Todd for the wonderful work that he does in helping us have hope, reach goals, and just know that life is not over. Perhaps it has just begun for some of us. Again, thank you Todd. I have another friend who I met because of my injury. I too am a quad in a wheelchair and I have a friend named Ken who is a respiratory therapist. When he was younger he had hopes of joining the military and becoming a ranger, but fate stepped in in the form of a motorcycle accident. He busted his knee and could not be accepted in the military. He had no thoughts of getting into the medical field or becoming a respiratory therapist, but God led him that way because God knew that his services would be needed to help people who are injured. I told him that God did not intend for him to be a ranger, but to be right where he is, in a rehabilitation center where he helps people who can't help themselves. Ken is very good at it and enjoys the reward, the feeling, and the love of helping other people. Above all this is what God wants us to do in our lives- helping one another, caring for one another. The strong should reach down and help the weak. So think about this- if your life is going in the direction that you think it should go but suddenly it takes a sharp turn, it may be God's way of redirecting you to do His will and not yours. It is very satisfying when you see a person recovering from an injury or is in distress and you are able to help them. Helping those who are weaker than you. This is a satisfaction and a feeling that no amount of money can buy. It strengthens your spirit, it gives you a desire to want to do more, it makes you stand just a little taller being able to help someone who needs it. So in closing I want to say again, God bless my two friends Todd and Ken for the wonderful work they do in the Lord's name to help other people.

Again my name is Jasper, all praise to the Lord.

March 13, 2014

COUNT IT ALL JOY

Hello my name is Jasper, all praises to the Lord.

I am a native of Detroit, Michigan and I've gotten used to the Michigan weather. Michigan weather can be very strange at times. Growing up in Detroit I've heard it said "if you don't like the weather, just wait a few minutes and it'll change". With all the storms we've been having lately across the country, Michigan has been suffering a lot of snow. I hear people complain about the frigid temperatures, about how tired they are of the snow, they're ready for the weather to break and can't wait till spring comes. All their feelings about the weather are valid, but I feel that God's people learn to take every day and everything that comes with that day in stride. I don't complain about the weather, how much snow falls, or how much rain comes down, because I'm just glad to still be here to see it. I remind myself that the Lord makes no mistakes. Whatever He decides to give us is good for us and He gives it to us for a reason. God controls the weather and this is His earth, not ours. He knows exactly what it means. Actually when the snow falls it's very beautiful. Just think, after a fresh summer rain does the earth smell good? It has a clean feeling about it as if God just pours down the rain and washes everything clean. The snow falls and covers the ground, and when it melts it saturates the earth with moisture to prepare the trees, and the flowers, and everything to flourish. God does not like for us to complain or be upset when He does something in the Earth. He said "count it all joy" because everything that He does He does it for our best interest. We may not understand the harsh weather, the earthquakes, the tidal waves, fires, etc. But remember; He also said "my thoughts are far above your thoughts, and my ways you cannot understand". We don't try to figure out why or how God does what he does, we just accept it, deal with it, and accept Him for who He is. Don't be so quick to complain about life's situations and conditions. God always does what is best for us.

My name is Jasper, praise Him.

April 1, 2014

FEED YOUR INNER SPIRIT

Hello my name is Jasper, praise Him He's worthy.
I was speaking with a young lady this morning and she was telling me that she had missed a lot of church lately. She had always been an active member in the church, but I suppose because of her work schedule she hasn't been able to go for quite a while. She said that she was kind of annoyed with herself because she got up and left the service. She felt that she just didn't want to be there. I thought about that and I told her that "if you believe in Jesus, then you have to believe in Satan because the scriptures speak of both". I said that Satan does not want us to go to church period. He does not want us to hear the word of God preached to us by the man of God. She said that if she doesn't go to church then the children don't go. I replied that's exactly what Satan wants. If he can stop you from going, then he also stops the children from going. He doesn't want them to be raised up in the word of God. It's just this simple- if you're not serving Jesus, then you're serving Satan. So you have to ask yourself, who is Lord over your life? Lord Jesus has a certain plan all mapped out for our lives. It is our duty to find out what that plan is and then carry it out. The only way that you can find out these things is to get as close to Him as you can. God said "I will give you pastors, and preachers, and teachers, and the like". It is not the man that you're actually listening to, but if he is a man of God it is God's word that is being spoken through him. The Bible states that "how can the people hear without a preacher?" Meaning He speaks to us all through the spirit, but He has

commissioned preachers, and pastors, to feed his people, His word. It is actually the word of God that you are listening to through the man of God. So I encourage you to put aside all these little petty things, like "I'm too tired", "I'll go next Sunday", "I don't feel like getting dressed", and all the excuses we make not to go. Remember, it is the enemy's job to keep you from the word of God. When you get active in the church and you're there on a regular basis, when you stop going you should feel something is wrong. You may feel like something is missing, and you're out of place. The word of God draws you closer to Him. He said in His word "I will reveal myself to those who diligently seek me". The more Jesus that you get inside you, the more of Him you will see. He will reveal himself to you. We need to be around people who believe the same things that you believe. We go to the church house to fellowship with believers like ourselves so that we can be on one accord. That is why the church is so divided today. Everybody wants to do something different. We have so many different denominations and different views on God's word, when actually it's all very plain and straight to the point if you search your Bible. This is what the enemy wants- the church to be divided. One against the other in the name of the Lord. What a mess. So read the scriptures for yourself. Read them over and over, for the more you read the better you'll understand. Find a good church home where they believe in practicing the scriptures, where they believe in rejoicing and honoring God for who He is. This is just my suggestion to you. Thank you, my name is Jasper, praise the Lord.

April 10, 2014

EXPECTATIONS

Hello my name is Jasper, praise the Lord.

Most of us can remember a time when we were expecting something to happen in our lives. When we were young kids at Christmastime we all expected to get the toy that we wanted. As we grew older we may have our first relationship, and we expect the girl or young man to like us. Often times we expect certain things from our job, or we may expect to be rewarded for good deeds that we've done. When we pray to the Lord we pray honestly, and we expect Him to give us what we're asking for. He is our Lord and our father, and like any good father when we do good and we're obedient, we expect our father to be good to us. Father God is no different. He wants to be good to us, He wants us to ask Him for things, He wants us to be obedient to Him so He can be good to us in return. There is absolutely nothing wrong with praying and expecting good results, but it takes strong faith. This is what pleases God. It is written "you cannot please God without faith". That is the one thing that He requires of us more than anything else. When we have strong faith in His word and we pray sincerely to Him, we should expect excellent results because He is a perfect God and He cannot lie. When He makes promises to us and we have faith, those promises will be kept. This should be a very exciting thing to know. This should be something that we can look forward to in our lives, just knowing that when we pray to God He will do what we ask Him to do, as long as we have faith in Him and are obedient to His word. So be of good cheer, for we have the Lord on our side and He will do exactly what He has promised. So I encourage you to take a good look at your faith, keep your spirits strong, and always trust in the Lord.

My name is Jasper, and He is worthy of all praise.

April 15, 2014

IT'S GOD'S WORLD

Hello my name is Jasper, peace and love.

As I go through the hallways of where I live, I hear lots of comments concerning the weather. Only a couple days ago the temperature had turned warm. As a matter of fact one day it hit the 70s. I remember because I went out to the doctor that day and I had taken my cap and jacket, and thinking I wish I had left both of them at home because it was so warm. But the very next day when I arose from my sleep, I realized what the weatherman predicted was true. It snowed the very next day and we actually broke a record. Here it is the middle of April and we broke a record with snowfall. I hear comments both of surprise and what a bummer the snow is, but using my inner spirit and focusing on God and who He is I'm just thankful to be here to see the snow. I'm thankful each day that I am here on earth to see whatever God brings my way. As I looked outside the pine trees and everything covered with snow- it was actually quite beautiful. Everything looked so clean and fresh with the fallen snow. It just confirms to me that God is still in control. He is showing us that this is His world, He alone controls the temperature. He alone controls the elements. He is showing us "it's my world and I do with it whatever I desire". Think about this- how can it be 70 degrees one day, and then it's snowing the very next day? Think about it. Only God can do that. Don't get so miffed about the weather or any other natural disaster, but remember God created this earth, and He is still in control of it. We may not always understand what He does, but He already told us. My thoughts are above yours as high as the heavens. We cannot figure out what God does or why, all we can do is stand still and know that He is God. You don't have to agree, but these are my thoughts.

Again my name is Jasper, peace and love to you.

April 29, 2014

WHERE YOU NEED TO BE

Hello my name is Jasper, praise the Lord.

I went recently to view my new apartment. This will be the first apartment of my own since my accident in April of '09. Since that time I've been living from the hospital to the rehab. I've lived in a wonderful rehab for some 5 years. I've had the blessing of good caring people, beautiful and clean surroundings, but I feel that now my spirit has moved me to go in another direction. As I'm thinking about my new apartment and how nice it is, and I believe I'll be cared for by more caring and committed people. As I thought more about this, what's going on in my life right now, I can see that none of this is my doing. I didn't have some great strategy to leave the rehab, but because of the supportive people that the Lord put in my life, all I had to do was point the direction I wanted to go and God has done the rest. Looking back at my past life I can see where He's always put me exactly where I needed to be. He's always given me the support that I've needed to go a step further. A supportive family, a supportive NA family. He guided me to a good solid church home where I could learn more about life, myself, and Him. When I had the accident yes it was a terrible thing, but again the Lord knew what He was doing. I could've died on the expressway that evening, but He allowed me to live. I had to go through a rough time but He changed my life and He brought me closer to Him. Before that I was running around too much, to spend quality time with Him. I believe He was displeased so He chastised me to bring me into submission to Him. But still He's always had me right where I needed to be. I made a decision that I will be willing to accept any challenge that He brings my way. That's why when I'm presented with new ideas, new paths to walk down, I readily accept because He wants me to live a fruitful life. Not to be held down by the cares of the world or bound down by drugs. He wants me to see life clearly and all the wonderful blessings that it has in store. That's why with the support of others I decided to write blogs, write a book, move to a new apartment, perhaps one day do public speaking, and do it all in His blessed name. Yes, I'm sure that if you look over your life you can see where the Lord has always had you right where you needed to be. When we look at our lives sometimes and we think it's falling apart, through God it's actually coming together. So I encourage you to keep reading the word, pray on a daily basis, and examine your life.

My name is Jasper, peace and love.

May 5, 2014

HE'S A PROVIDER

Hello my name is Jasper, all praises to the Lord.

First of all I would like to start by saying that life is a precious gift given to us by our Lord and Savior. It's not to be taken lightly, it's not to be taken for granted, but it is to be appreciated and savored like a splendid meal. He wants us to enjoy it and all that He requires of us is to recognize Him for who He is. He's our Heavenly Father, we are His children, and He provides for us everything we need. I was thinking about that as I was meditating and reflecting on my life, thinking about the rehab center where I live, take my therapy sessions, interact with all the wonderful people who work there. I had no idea that I would have an accident on April 28th, 2009 that would change my life completely. But God knew, that's why He provided me with the insurance that I needed to be where I am today. I had only gotten the insurance perhaps a week or so before my accident. He provided care for me when I was in the ICU, He provided care for me in my first rehab, and then He sent me to a place called Special Tree where I began to learn some things, not only about my condition, but about myself as a person. Well I've been here for almost 5 years and in that time He has put many people in my life that have helped carry me to the next level. He also guided me to a new church home where I began to learn different things about Him that I had never been taught before. He has brought to me new challenges, and a new excitement about things that ought to come in my life. So I will be leaving the rehab center and going to my own apartment. He has provided for me a remodeled apartment with all brand new appliances, He has provided for me a full staff that will be with me 24/7, He has provided for me food and money that I can use toward my living expenses. Yes as I look over my life I can see where my Father provides for me everything I need. I see the obvious- I'm in a wheelchair and I'm pretty much physically helpless. I cannot do for myself but He, who is the great provider, gives me everything and everyone that I need. So as it says in the scriptures don't worry about what you shall eat, or what you shall wear, He said the Father takes care of the sparrow, and He cares for you much more than the sparrow. So why should you worry or have concern for your being? He will provide for you because you are His child, and like any good father He only wants what is best for you. So I say to you- learn of Him, learn what He requires of you, be obedient to His word, hear the word, believe the word, and then act upon the word, and you will be blessed.

My name is Jasper, praise the Lord.

May 12, 2014

HOW TO LIVE A LONG LIFE

Hello my name is Jasper, bless the Lord.

How many of us desire to live a long and fruitful life? Do we dream of days on the front porch with the swing in the summer breeze? Do we see ourselves playing with our grandchildren or our great-grandchildren? Do we see ourselves being thankful for the long and good life that the Lord has blessed us with? Well, if you take a look at Psalm 34:12 you will see what the Lord requires of you that He may bless you with a long and fruitful life. It's nothing really difficult, it's quite simple for the righteous man. He says, what man desires a long and prosperous life? The first thing you must do is watch the things that come out of your mouth. We must be reminded that words are a living thing and they can build you up or they can tear you down. Be aware of every word that you spring forth from your mouth. Is it to do good? Or is it to do evil? The second thing He requires is that you watch your behavior. Remember, you are a minister or representative of the most high God. He expects you to carry yourself in a righteous manner. He expects you to be holy because He is holy. Be aware of where you go and how you act. Be aware of how you conduct yourself with others. When people see you they should see the God spirit that lives in you. And finally, He says be a peace maker. Seek peace and go after it. Peace will not always come to you, you must seek it, go after it, and pursue it. Always be quick to understand and be tolerant of others, and slow to anger. Do these things and you will find that the Lord will bless you with a long and fruitful life. Who wants to live a long life if it's not going to be good and fruitful to you? No one in their right mind would want to live a long life filled with misery. Do these things of the Lord, and He will bless you with your heart's desire.

Goodbye, my name is Jasper.

May 19, 2014

FAMILY

Hello my name is Jasper, praise God.

I live in a very nice rehabilitation center due to an auto accident. The accident changed my life drastically, whereas I could no longer live life as I used to. I literally have to depend on someone else to do even the most simple of tasks. It is a very humbling experience to have to depend on someone for everything. But God is still good, and as He promised He's always provided me with everything that I need. I recently had a very nice visit from two of my daughters and four of my grandchildren. As I talked with them and played with my grandkids I once again began to realize how wonderful life can be. Life is a gift from God and the gift is very fragile and should not be taken lightly. In my opinion enjoy as much as your life as you can, while you can, as often as you can. God, who created both Heaven and Earth, also invented marriage. From that marriage is supposed to spring forth offspring, which produces a family. God created family not only to fill the earth, but also to be able to love and take care of one another. It makes me feel so wonderful when my daughters express so much concern for their father. They are quick to come to my aid, help me with all my decisions, and now that I'm in this condition they literally take care of me. I believe that's one reason God created family. To love and care and support one another. Siblings create by instinct a natural bond with one another. Children usually take care of their parents as they grow old, just as their parents took care of them when they were young. Family is something that you just strive to do your best for, to provide, to protect, to nurture, to understand, be tolerant, and instill in your family all the qualities which make up a decent human being. You will find as you grow older and your understanding broadens, that without family you drift alone. Your family is like an anchor that keeps you centered in this vast world of ours. To watch your family grow before your very eyes, to watch the nurturing blossom, to watch the love become overflowing is such a beautiful thing. It is truly what life is all about. It is a holy thing, given to us by God himself, to take care of just as He took care of us and is still doing so. There is nothing to compare with the love of family. So next time when you're at the family picnic or the family reunion, or just sitting at the kitchen table helping your child with their homework, take notice to the feelings that you get. That good feeling of joy and the feeling of accomplishment, knowing that you're a vital part of the family. Fathers- take care of your family and God will be ever mindful to bless you for it.

Thank you for reading, my name is Jasper, praise the Lord.

May 27, 2014

LETTING GO

Hello brothers and sisters, praise be to the Lord.

My name is Jasper and I'm going to a funeral this week to bury a lady that was like a mother to me. We used to work together for the Detroit school board as custodians. I was in a real low point in my life at that time due to crack addiction. I was surviving any way that I could, even taking lunches out at the garbage cans that kids had thrown away. I didn't know it because she never told me, but she saw me taking those lunches from the garbage and so she began to bring extra food for lunch so I wouldn't do that. We ate lunch and we talked and she helped me in a lot of ways without me even knowing that she was helping me. We became real close and I jokingly told her that she reminded me of my mother. She acted like my mother, she talked like my mother, and she cussed like my mother. And so a friendship and a bond developed. She was like a mother to me and I was like a son to her. She took me in when I had no place to go, she fed me when I was hungry, and she looked out for me in so many ways. You see, I believe God's word is true because in this life of ours He said "I will always give you what you need". Sometimes as we go through our lives He'll give us who we need. Today I have so many friends that walk in the light of the Lord. We talk to each other, we strengthen each other, they have never looked down on me when I was at my lowest. I'm going to bury my second mother this week, but it does not bother me because I know that she obeyed the Lord. She had the spirit of the Lord

inside her, and she did His will. So I know that I will see her once again in paradise. The Lord has put many people in my life that I need, for instance I'm transitioning to an apartment of my own. I'm a quadriplegic so physically there's nothing I can do, and being in a wheelchair I'm somewhat limited to where I can go, but the Lord sent the right people to me to get done what I need to have done. I barely opened my mouth and told someone what I wanted, then they got their people online and before I knew it I was making the transition to my apartment. To show you when the Lord has something for you, nothing can stop it. The insurance company said the apartment was too expensive, they did not want to pay for it. But the people working for me negotiated with them, made some deals, and I got the apartment at a reduced rate. Everything in the apartment (all the appliances) is brand new, I will have a 24 hour staff, and also I had to give up the transportation that the complex provided. They will take you anywhere you want to go within a 10 mile radius, but I cannot use that. So what did the Lord do? He got someone to donate a van for me free of charge, and all I have to do is have the aid and a nurse with me and they will drive me anywhere I want to go. When the Lord has something for you, it's going to be just what you need. He will provide. So my message to you is don't worry about anything, be not anxious for anything, but wait on the Lord. Ask for what you want, and I guarantee His word is true. He will give it to you. So be blessed, pray, and don't worry.
My name is Jasper, and these are my thoughts.

September 26, 2014

HE'LL DO IT FOR YOU

Hello, My name is Jasper. All praises to the Lord. I came across an interesting story, one of encouragement, love, and the power of our Lord. He loves us all. He does things for us that we cannot do for ourselves because he has a purpose for our lives. This is a testimony about a little boy around the age of 8 who was at a pool party. At the party, some of his friends were having a lot of fun in the shallow end of the pool. He decided to join them and he dived into the water, head first, but he struck his head on the bottom of the pool breaking his neck in 4 places. He broke it from the first column to the fourth column and when the doctors examined him they informed his parents that most people with this type of injury do not recover. Still, they air lifted the little boy to another hospital where special doctors could attend to him. His father was very distraught, he didn't know what to do, he was a wreck. All he could do was just pray, hold his hands up to his head, and pray to the Lord. The boy's mother began to talk to her relatives. The relatives, in turn, began to tell their friends about the incident. The friends began to share this tragedy with their church and before long there was a huge prayer vigil for this young man. The parents were awaiting news of his condition. They had to wait a little while because he was in another city. When they got news of his condition, they were told not only did he live, but he fully recovered. He actually recovered to the point where he did not need to see any physical therapists or have any physical therapy. To me, this is a modern day miracle. What once was, is no more. God completely turned the situation around. I want you to be encouraged today, saints. If God will do it for this little boy, in your times of trouble, he will also do it for you. He is the same yesterday, today, and tomorrow. He said "I will always be with you, even until the end of time. Just have faith and believe in me and I will take care of you." He is a God that cannot lie. Keep this in mind as you go through your life struggles. God is always there just waiting for you to ask for help. My name is Jasper. He is worthy of all praise.

October 20, 2014

WALKING ALONG WITH JESUS

Hello my name is Jasper,
All praises to the Lord. Sometimes in life we are put in the position that may seem overwhelming. We may not know how to handle it or which way to turn. It seems as though we can't get any help that we need, but something in our spirit causes us to press on and persevere. We seem to be driven towards this goal no matter how much opposition we may encounter. I'd like to speak about one such young lady, Malala, she is from Pakistan and is only seventeen years old. In Pakistan, the woman have very few rights if any. She was not allowed to attend school, although it was in her heart to do so anyway. They went to great lengths to stop her, they even shot her in the head. After she recovered, she went right back to her goal of going to school. So a lot of things transpired for her, and she ended up winning the Nobel Piece Prize for her efforts. She is the youngest to ever win the coveted prize. I just know that the Lord was with her, and God's spirit she has inside of her pushed her towards her goal. I'd like to speak about another incident, or should I say another miracle that the Lord has shown us. I believe that the Lord sends us messages through miracles, if we have eyes to see. There was a young man who was a racecar driver. Needless to say, this is a dangerous sport, and on a certain day, it seemed the worst happened to him. He lost control of his car and had a terrible crash. It seemed that looking at the car and crash, no one could possibly survive the outcome. They pulled this young man from the wreckage, he did his time in the hospital, he was

broken up from head to toe (his collarbone, legs, neck). He was a broken mess. His parents prayed for him day and night, of course, that was their son. Sometimes God puts you a position where no one can seem to help you, and all you can think of to do, is to pray to the creator. The one who started it all, the creator of heaven and earth, and all that dwells within. Well, I'm not sure how long it took, but the Lord must have heard their cries, because I was watching a TV show where I got this story, and that man walked on this show and he looked like he had never been in a car crash in his whole life. In my opinion, that can only be the grace of God. I've been a quadriplegic for a little over five years, physically I can do nothing for myself, I'm not rich by any means, I don't have any degrees, I don't come from a wealthy family, I'm just an average man. But, I believe in the Lord and what he says. I believe in his word, his word is true. He is taking care of me, better than I could take care of myself. Whatever I have asked for, I've gotten it. I have a nice apartment to live in, when transportation was not available to me anymore, someone I've never met stepped up and donated their van so I could make my appointments. I did not ask for any of that. That is called God's grace! He gave me things that he knows I need without even asking. Because he is a God that can not lie, and he said "If you obey me, if you worship me, I will supply all of your needs. Look first, to the kingdom of Christ, and be steadfast, and all these things should be added to you." Don't worry about anything, just serve the Lord, and he will provide and take care of you. My name is Jasper, and I am a believer! Be blessed and be a blessing to someone.

November 13, 2014

THANKSGIVING LOVE

Hello my name is Jasper,

I greet you in the name of my Lord and savior Jesus Christ. It looks as though the Thanksgiving holiday is here once again. What do you think of when you think of Thanksgiving? A lot of people think of how beautiful the fall season is with all of the bright colored leaves. God paints a beautiful picture for us in the fall season. Some people think of Christmas being just around the corner. Their minds are filled with how much am I going to do this year? Who do I have to buy for? They seem to be rushing around already from store to store. But me, when I think of Thanksgiving, I think of a warm, cozy home filled with wonderful smells of food and family fun. It's a time when family has time to come together and break bread and give thanks to the lord for the life he has given you. Even the word, "Thanks-giving," means give thanks for what you already have. Give thanks to the Lord for what he has done already or will do for you. Take time to pray together with your family and give thanks. It's a time to teach the little children about giving thanks and the joy of giving period. Giving of yourself, giving someone a gift when you don't have to. Thanksgiving should be a time when family comes together and loves on one another. Just eating your fill, having fun with your loved ones, and your family and being joyous. Looking forward to the new year and knowing that the almighty is on your side. That's what Thanksgiving means to me.

November 20, 2014

IT'S NEVER THAT BAD

Hello my name is Jasper, and I greet you in the blessed name of Jesus, who is the head of my life. I love to go to the movies, I went to a movie last night and it started me to thinking the next day. The whole story started with this beautiful young woman with the world at her feet, everything to live for, but yet she tried to commit suicide. Her life to her had become so horrible, so painful, so hopeless, that she no longer wanted to live. You have teenagers committing suicide at a rapid rate today. You have people committing suicide for all sorts of reasons. But my brothers and sisters, I remind you the Lord said, "There is no situation that you can get yourself into that I have not provided a way out for you." Life should never reach a point for you where you want to end your own life. I'm sure it might feel that way at the moment because that's what the enemy wants you to feel. He wants you to feel hopeless, degraded, that there is no need to go on. BUT I say to you, the Lord your God created you for a purpose, and he will not let anything take you away from this world until you have fulfilled this purpose. So I say stop, stand still, and when you don't know what to do, don't do anything, but stop and listen. You will hear that voice come to you inside, the spirit that lives inside of you, is greater than the spirit that lives in the world. He will guide you and lead you to where you want to be. You have to have the strength and faith to hold on. My story is short and quick to the point today. Don't listen to the enemy. Don't be deceived, he is the author of the lie. Don't listen to him, instead, read your bible and find out what the true word of God is. Once you learn that, you have no need to fear the enemy. He has already been defeated when Jesus went to the cross for us. My name is Jasper. Love you.

2015

February 17, 2015

GOING THROUGH

Hello my name is Jasper,
We all go through difficult times, and get into difficult circumstances for some of us the situation seems hopeless. I am a quadriplegic so I have had these feelings that things wont turn out good for me at the end of the day, but then I am reminded of who I belong to, and who I am in life. The lord does not bring you to a certain level or certain point, and then leave you hanging as he said in his word, I will never leave you nor forsake you. So we should be reminded of that when going through difficult times. We must have faith, and believe that no matter what the circumstance may be it will all come out good for you in the end. He loves us dearly and he does not take us through bad times to punish us, but he is always teaching. Sometimes for some people they have to go through something, experience it first hand before they see the big picture, I know this all too well because I am also an addict. I went through years of hardship, low self esteem, and confusion, and it remained that way until the lord put me in a situation where I could slow down, and really see what life is all about. He put me in a situation so I could be closer to him than I ever been before. When you're in a wheelchair and you don't have the use of your body, only your mind, your mouth, and your heart, you will think about the lord. Playtime is over, and it is time to be serious about your life. The lord showed me that life itself is a precious gift it is not to be abused,

taken for granted, you should live each moment as though it was the last, and don't forget to pray to him give him all the credit, all the glory, and worship that you can. That is all he requires of us, is that we believe in him and worship, have faith in him, and live a holy life, if you can do this I guarantee you, he will bless you at the end of the day. I have had many wonderful things happen to me and the way they happen I know it had to be the lord. He did things for me that I could not do for myself he showed me favor when I didn't deserve it, and I thank him, and I praise him, and I place his name above all other names. Lord Jesus he is truly the lord of my life, make him the lord of your life he will guide your steps, open doors for you, and he will open your eyes to the truth. Again, my name is Jasper, be blessed, and be a blessing to someone.

March 3, 2015

TOUGH TIMES

Hello, my name is Jasper and I want to talk about the tough times in our lives. Tough times, have you ever wondered or felt like you were the only one going through something, you may even ask why me ? Why am I having such a rough time? Nothing seems to work for me, like it does for other people. You may be an individual that has come to a point in your life where your back is totally against the wall, no friends, no family, no income, and no one to come and save you. We all go through tough times in our lives, but I believe we do for a reason. The lord does not make your life rough for you on purpose. He loves us too much, to make us suffer, but he will allow you to experience some feelings from your situation. He watches over us, and he always teaches us a lesson in life. He knows you will not listen to anybody, and you believe you can do it all on your own, so he allows you to go through a tough time to remind you, that you're just human and you dont really control anything, but he knows when you've lost that job, stressed out because you cant pay bills, lost your new car, wife wants to leave, you and some individuals may have to go through all of this before they think of Him. Even though you're going through something like that he is still with you, just waiting for you to say lord help me. I know I cant go on like this, I have nowhere else to turn, so now I am asking you please hear my cry, and have faith after your prayer and he will surely turn things around for you. Sometimes we human beings get arrogant and stubborn, and think we're better than everyone else. The lord frowns on pride, because the wisest man who ever lived said that pride goes before a fall. So when you have too much pride in yourself look out, you're going to start messing up somewhere down the road. When the lord blesses you with something, be humble and thankful, because he is showing you favor that you do not deserve. We mess up sometimes and do things we know we shouldnt do, but when we ask him he is quick to forgive, and we should thank him from the bottom of our hearts, for showing us grace and mercy. So in your walk through life when you come to a situation where you find yourself going through a difficult time, consider it all to be joy. It is just the lords way of building your character, making you strong, keeping you humble, and do not worry he is still in control of your situation. Just be strong, steadfast, keep your faith, and he will pick you up and put you where you need to be. I tell you this brothers and sisters hoping it will strengthen your faith, because I've been there. I have had my back touch the wall many times, many times I did not know where my next meal would come from. I was locked into a lifestyle that I could not shake off, but the lord was with me all through my situation. He fed me, he kept a roof over my head, he put caring people in my life, and he pulled me through. Trust in him, and he will do the same for you. Again, my name is Jasper and I love you.

March 26, 2015

AS FOR ME AND MY HOUSE…. WE WILL SERVE THE LORD

Hello, my name is Jasper, a lot of people are going through their lives today, lost in a world of confusion, frightened, and not knowing where to turn. The children seem unruly, you're stressed on your job, there is always a lack of provisions in your home. You have husbands who don't know how to care for their wives, and you have wives who don't know how to hold on to their husbands. The reason these things happen in your life is because you don't know Lord Jesus. When you don't know the lord, you run around doing unnecessary things and often times you're out of control and don't even know it. If the husband who is the head of the family is getting his direction from the lord he'll know how to treat, and care for his wife. Infidelity won't cross his mind, he'll enjoy going to work everyday to care for his family. He won't run the streets and get drunk, do drugs, but rather he'll find his pleasure where his heart is, at home. It is written, he that finds a wife, finds a good thing. He will recognize and appreciate that, in finding his wife. A lot of men don't even realize when they have been blessed with the wife from the lord. A lot of women and wives don't like the idea of following the desires of her husband. They seem to want to defy him at every turn. The husband is who the lord holds responsible if the marriage fails. It is hard to be a leader of something if your followers won't follow you, but when a wife is willing to submit to her husband, support him, follow him, she is also following the lord, and in turn what she learns from the lord she will pour into the children. The end result is you have a Christian household, and the entire house will be blessed. When you follow the lord your problems do not seem that bad. He will fill every void in your life. Your wife will be good to you, because you're good to her. Jesus will give you patients, tolerance, understanding, empathy for another person, and most of all peace and understanding. It is written, the fear of the lord is the beginning of knowledge, that is why those who do not know him are not as smart as they think. So live your life the way you see fit. Do all those things that to you see as important, but as for me and my house, we will serve the lord. Again, my name is Jasper, God bless.

April 7, 2015

WHY NOT LET GO

Hello my name is Jasper, and I do love you. Have you ever watched a cowboy movie and they're dragging a man behind a running horse? He goes from so much dirt and thorns and he gets hurt because the horse is dragging him so fast , well that is the way some of us live our lives... As if we're being dragged by a running horse. We can't seem to stop, despite the pain we are going through. We have no control over our lives as we zig-zag from one thing to another. Well just like that cowboy if you could only let go, you would stop hurting, you would regain control of your life, and you would have a chance to stand up and view life clearly. What I am saying is if you're in turmoil and confusion just let go, and let God handle things. He knows the beginning and the end of fate. He will guide us through the wilderness of this world, as he said in his word I will always give you what you need! We must learn to believe that, and look for it in our lives. I have watched how he has taken care of some of my friends, and it has made my faith stronger. I have known people to let go of a job, relocate, may be even have to cut someone out of their life, but just let go of whatever is hurting you, and give it to God. I want to speak more about marriage...there would be less trouble between husband and wife if they would just let go of these jealous feelings, envy, selfishness, being stubborn, and let God's word show you how to take care of your spouse. A husband is supposed to be head of the household, he should not be a wimp, but also not controlling. His wife is a gift from God. She will always help him, if he allows her to. He should not be so headstrong, that he wont listen to his wife. God gave her certain abilities and she can sense things that you can't! Often times your wife will feel something before it happens, and she may try to worn you, but your male ego won't allow you to listen, then you have to come back after you fell into the pit that she tried to warn you of, with your head down saying and I quote "yes dear you were right all along". She should feel protected by you she should feel secure and content. Husbands should learn first how to take care of a woman before you marry one. Now wives, you also should learn how to care of your husband. You should get to know him, study him, learn his moves, likes and dislikes. A smart wife knows her position and her power, and she knows in her own way how to get her husband to do exactly what she wants. She knows that she is smarter than he is without letting him know it. She has love for her husband, she is not his enemy, but rather a valuable asset to him. She knows how to step back and allow him to be the man, and still hold her head high. As my mother used to say "tongue and teeth fall out with each other sometimes, but they still exist in the same mouth". A husband and wife must realize that everyday may not be sunny and bright, but when you go through the storm together, supporting one another, and trusting God you become stronger. I am just trying to make a point that instead of always putting your mate down, back stabbing them, manipulating them, you should support them. Love, understanding, commitment, honesty, these are a few of the tools that will provide a healthy marriage. These things are just my opinion, some of them are my life's experience. I just want to help you get through some of the rough spots, you will encounter in your marriage, but if you ever get discouraged, doubtful, or unsure, remember let go and let God handle it. Again, my name is Jasper be blessed.

April 30, 2015

MY FRIEND

Exactly, what is a friend? What does the term "friend" mean to you? In my opinion a friend is someone that sticks close to you, who understands you, you have a kindred spirit with your friend, they're not judgemental or envious, nor jealous of you. When you have successful blessings in your life, they're not jealous, they are happy with your success. A friend is someone who is willing to tell you when you're wrong, or when you're making a mistake. They don't do it to be difficult but rather to help you from getting into a bad situation. A true friend is one who is quick to come to your aid. No matter what the circumstances they are with you. That is the way it is with Jesus. He will stay closer to you than any brother. He will always come to you in your worst of times. He will not judge you, but He is there to help you and comfort you. There is a song that says "what a good friend we have in Jesus". That is so true! You could not have a better friend in your life. Knowing that He is always there and He will never leave you or foresake you. When you're at your lowest point He does not shy away from you, but He waits eagerly for you to ask Him for help. We must always bear this in mind, because we go through so many hills and valleys in our life that we need someone to give us hope, and a desire to press on. That hope is in Christ Jesus. He will watch you as you go through your troubles, He's always teaching you even in your struggles, that after you have suffered a while He won't let you suffer more than you can bear. He will pick you up, dust you off, turn you around, and put you back where you belong. He will settle you, strengthen you, and re-establish you. It should feel good knowing that you have a friend like this. We should strive to be the same way towards our friends. We should be supportive, not judgemental, and always have a heart to love and support. This is the way Christ wants us to live and get along with each other. If we love each other the way Christ has loved us, He said there will be a reward at the end of it all.

Blessings to everyone, Jasper.

May 14, 2015

HOW IS YOUR LIFE?

Most people desire to have a happy and fruitful life. They wish to live long, watch their kids grow up, and enjoy life in general. But sometimes it's not that easy. There are forces of darkness that seem to interrupt us. Believe it or not, there was an angel in Heaven that was named Lucifer. Lucifer was allowed in the throne room with God himself. He was the most beautiful angel, he was so beautiful that when he walked beautiful music would play. But then he began to get beside himself, even thinking that he was equal with God. Soon, he began to think himself better than God. He was banished from Heaven and one third of the angels who followed him went with him. He is present in the earth, and he hates God, so he causes all kinds of damage and mayhem in our lives. He does this because he knows that we are God's creation, and God loves us. He goes about the business of making us unhappy, trying to ruin our lives. He will make us do things to ourselves, or even kills us. He can only do this by influencing us to do things to ourselves. He has no real power because the Lord defeated him by going to the cross. He would kill us all if he could, but he can't because God won't let him. Although he has some power, don't take him for granted, but we don't have to fear him because God did not give us the spirit of fear. We have the Lord Jesus on our side to fight for us. Lucifer, who is sometimes called Satan, tried to use Jesus in the wilderness. But Jesus defeated him by using scripture against him. We have the power to do the same. When you feel in your mind you want to do something that you know you should not do, just call on the Lord and He will give you strength to defeat Satan's attack. Satan's spirit is no match for the God spirit that Jesus put in us. We have to learn how to use the spirit inside of us, when to call on Him for strength and guidance. We must first of all believe and understand that He is the living Son of God. Anything that we desire to do that is good comes from our Jesus spirit that's inside of us. Things like compassion, understanding, meekness, love for your brother- these are the things of God. Lord Jesus promised us if we keep His commandments, we will live a long and productive life. He will keep the enemy away from us. He will increase our faith, and we will be heirs of the kingdom with Him. Satan knows this, so he tries to make us do things that are against God's word. So I ask you, how is your life? Take a look at your life and see, is it prosperous? Or is it always in turmoil? If things seem to always go against you, or you seem to hurt people and do wrong things, you're following Satan. If you have happiness and joy, love and apathy for someone else, you're serving the Lord. So take a close look at your life, and decide who you are serving, and remember you can't serve two masters.

July 1, 2015

SAME SEX MARRIAGES

Hello, my name is Jasper and I have some concerns about what our government is allowing into society. To anyone who has read my blogs before, you know that my messages are about Christian values. I don't wish to offend anyone, any particular group or society of people. I feel that I should say something regarding the society of Jesus Christ. Sometimes we all want to do our own thing, we want to do what we want to do and no one is going to stop us. But the society I belong to are followers of Christ. We give our will and our lives over to him. We profess to be his followers by doing exactly as he commands. His thoughts and his doctrines are the only laws that truly matter to us, for he is supreme. We may not always agree with what his word says, we may not like what he asks us to do sometimes, but at the end of the day, we know we believe that whatever he commands, is all for our good. So when God says that homosexuality is a sin in his eyes and it shall not be tolerated, this is the law that we must abide by. Now some people get that all twisted around. They say, "well, God loves all people", some say there is no God, while others feel that God will love them no matter what. Homosexuality is a sin to the Father. It always has been, it is today, and it always will be, for his word and his will for us does not change. He does not hate the homosexual or the lesbian or anyone with an alternative lifestyle. He does love everyone, for we are his children, but he hates the act that some of us perform. He hates the things that we do behind closed doors when we feel that no one is watching. But the

Lord is omnipresent, meaning he is everywhere, he is everything, and we cannot hide from his eyes. And whether you believe it or not, he says one day you will have to come into judgement. He will sit at the right hand of the Father and he will judge us one and all. He will not only judge the big things in our lives, he will also judge those tiny little sins that we thought didn't matter. When Jesus walked this Earth and he interacted with us and our lust for sins he became our go-between with the Father. God the Father cannot look upon sin so Jesus stands in the gap for us, we are filled with his spirit and that is what God sees when he looks upon us. He does not see the ugliness of the sin in us but rather, the spirit of his son who is sinless.

So you make up your own minds what you want to do with your life, but remember this: what if there is a heaven and a hell and you find out too late that you've followed the wrong path? But by the time you find out then it will be too late. So why not take out some insurance and give your life to God and live the way he intended you to? Do the best you can, we all fall short sometimes, but the Lord knows your heart. He knows when you're giving it your best. He will not look down on you, he will not judge you, he will not hurt you in anyway, but he will cover you with his blood so that the enemy cannot destroy you. The enemy is someone who hates God. He hates us because of God. He is powerful and he will do anything he can to kill us. He cannot do this directly, but he will whisper to your mind and cause you to live a life that is against God's wishes. He will drag your life through the mud. And he will steal all your joy. His only purpose on this Earth is to steal, kill, and destroy. Don't let him ruin your life as he did mine for years, before I decided to truly follow Christ, give yourself a chance. The Lord said he will never leave us nor forsake us, but the enemy will always leave you in a mess that he got you into. I am only trying to give you some food for spiritual thought. Look over your life and see if you can tell the times when the lord was helping you and when the enemy was stealing your joy. Again, my name is Jasper, I love you all, and be blessed.

July 16, 2015

THINK.

Hello, my name is Jasper. I am a quadriplegic and a disciple of Christ. What do you think about in the course of a day? What do you think about when you are all alone and the room is quiet? Maybe your family, your social status, or perhaps it's your job? We have many commitments and obligations to meet in today's world. That takes up a lot of our thought process- just trying to keep up on society's freeway. We have so many things that we see as being so important we can't overlook them.But tell me, how much time in your daily routine do you take out to think about God? Do you think about the sacrifice that he made for us and what he commands us to do for one another? Do you think about helping someone whose life is not as good as yours? Perhaps you may know someone in financial or emotional distress, do you offer any help? Do we think about the fatherless children and the widow who has no husband to lean upon? Christ says that we are to love one another as he has loved us. We are to be a father to the fatherless, mother to the motherless, and don't forget about the old people who are just trying to make it day by day.Be honest with yourself. Do you show any real concern for people like this? Or do you just pass them by as if they don't exist? When you see a homeless person on the street, do you turn your head or do you ever think "there but for the grace of God, go I". These things should cross your mind on a daily basis. It's part of what makes us human, it's called empathy that understanding and concern for what the other person may be going through. If you want your life to be happy, prosperous, and joy filled, just start doing things to help other people. Don't forget about the less fortunate, and pull your brother up to your level. Don't just turn your head and do nothing. You can only get out of life what you put in. If you put in nothing, then nothing is what you will receive. This is just a short message to give you and idea of what your mind should be on. Reset your mind not to be selfish, not to be evil, and above all, not to forget God.

July 30, 2015

JESUS AND YOU

Hello, my name is Jasper. I pray that you are being blessed and all is well with you. I once heard a preacher say that when he first gave his life to the Lord, he thought the Lord didn't want him to have any fun. He said, " Now Lord, you mean I can't go to the bar, I can't go to the gentleman clubs, I can't have sex outside of marriage, you don't want me to gamble, if I tell a lie, you are mad at me? It seems that you don't want me to have any fun, do the things that I'm used to doing, I'll have to change my whole life!" Well that is exactly what the Lord wants you to do. like any good father, no matter how much fun a child is having, your father knows when you've had enough. You don't want to stop and you can;t see what you're doing, but your father loves you, has to calm you down, slow you down, and give you a new perspective. Father God wants us to enjoy this world but he doesn't want you to hurt yourself in the process. His commandments are not set forth to hinder you, but rather to help you and lift you up. No fornication means you don't have to worry about STD's or getting into any love triangles. Staying out of bars and clubs is a good thing because its full of people with a lot of bad habits. Drinking and doing drugs does not add to your life, it only takes away. That's why Jesus said "do not touch the unclean thing". He said "be ye holy for I am holy". Thats an order to give you some type of goal to shoot for that will strengthen you, keep you away from negative things. He also said do not do as the world does because the world can be cold, hearts waxed over, and man loves himself and does not care about his brother. But when you give your life to Christ, he teaches us that we must be humble and caring and unselfish towards our brothers and sisters. If you are planning on marriage in the near future, plan on following Jesus and I guarantee you your marriage will be positive and fruitful. There is no other correct way to live your life except to follow the law of the Lord. This is just a note to give you some food for thought. The Lord does not want to slow you down or take the fun out of your life, but rather to give you more life so you can have more fun. Again, my name is Jasper, may God bless you.

August 10, 2015

WHAT WE DON'T SEE

Hello, my name is Jasper and I am a minister for the Lord. There are things that are happening around us all the time that we know about but we cannot see. Trees grow strong and tall, but we don't see them grow, or see the growth process that goes on under the tree. We can feel the wind brush across our face, but we can't see what propels it and moves it along. I am a quadriplegic and like many others, I know my limbs are there even though I can't feel them. Many things happen in our daily lives that we do not understand. I want to go somewhere with this and get you to see there are many things going on and we don't know why. As one person told me, it's kind of like a baby in its mother's womb. That baby rests instinctively safe, not knowing who feeds it, where the care comes from. It just knows it happens. There is a force or person outside of that baby's comprehension. It can't see its mother but somehow the baby knows she's there. When you think of it, it's kind of that way with a christian. No, we've never seen God, but we feel his presence at all times. We feel secure in the knowledge that there is someone much bigger than ourselves, much greater than ourselves, who sustains us. Scientists are men of logic but there are even some things that happen in life, nature that even they cannot explain. They have searched the ruins and found evidence that there was a man named Jesus who walked this Earth. No, we cannot see him today, but he wants us to believe in him anyway. I have seen evidence in my life of a higher authority, although I've never seen him. I could feel it inside of me that spiritual battle that goes on inside of me. I have had my mind set on doing something I know is right, but my mind convinces me to do the opposite and when that happens, there is a strange feeling I get inside as though I can feel someone saying, "See, I got you again!". Other times, when I have that battle, and I am thinking of doing something I shouldn't when I resist it, the feeling says, "I'm so glad I didn't". It feels as thought there are two people in a tug-of-war and I am in the middle of he rope. I'm being flung back and forth. Sometimes winning, sometimes losing. Just because I can't see this battle, or see who is doing it, does not mean it's not happening to the believer. We know this all too real. So, I have learned to do what is necessary to stay on the right side of the battle field. Let me ask you, have you ever decided to go one place and then "something" suddenly changed your mind? You say to yourself later on, "I don't know why I did that, I just did". Or, have you ever meant to say one thing that you felt was the right thing to say, but something else came out? You scratch your head and think to yourself , "why did I say that"? Well my friend, whether you believe or not, there are two forces working in your life at all times. You cannot see them, but if you pay attention, you can feel their effects. So I urge you to just try the holy way of life. For Jesus said, "be ye holy because I am holy". Be aware of the things you cannot see. Trust me, they are there. Again, my name is Jasper, may God bless.

August 20, 2015

HOW'S YOUR DAY?

Hello my name is Jasper, and I pray that all is well with you.

I woke up this morning feeling good, in a very positive mood, and as I started my day I started speaking to people as I rolled down the hallway. I live in a neuro rehab center so I see a lot of people (clients, staff, and visitors). I try to speak to everyone I meet and I like to project a happy feeling. Often times if I don't feel that good inside or if I'm feeling kind of crappy myself, I don't let others see it. I could be in one of those places where I don't want to be bothered by anyone, but when someone speaks to me or smiles at me I automatically put on that face. It doesn't take a whole lot for you to smile and say "hello", even if you don't feel like doing it or talking to anyone. Just smile or nod and say "hello". In other words, always be uplifting and encouraging to your brother. Sometimes you don't know what the next person is going through. You don't know what emotional state they may be in, and that simple smile or that "hello" would just bring them out of that self-pity. That hug that you give someone may be the only love that they've felt in a long time, you just don't know. When we show love to our brother (and that includes women), we're doing what God asks us to do. Jesus said "love ye one another as I have loved you". It's my way of being happy for myself, no matter what my condition is. When I look out and I see all the green trees, the beautiful blue sky, just being able to open my eyes and see anything is a blessing. I just look all around me and I see the beautiful portrait that God has painted for me. I think about each breath that I take, my eyesight, being able to breathe, and of course watching my family grow up. I've often thanked God for allowing me to live long enough to watch my babies grow up, and then watch my babies' babies grow up. Nothing feels as good as having your children around you, and you're holding their children in your arms. You can't help but feel thankful and blessed that you're here to do that. I didn't always live such a safe and comfortable life. I am a recovering addict, and I've been lost in darkness many times. So I look at where I am today and I know it wasn't me that got me here. I tried to self-destruct many times, I filled my life with misery, but God still had favor with me and He guided me through my wilderness. He brought me out and reestablished me. That's not to say I didn't go through some tough times. I had a wife that I had to bury, I lost many a job, never stayed in one place very long, and as I said earlier I live in a neuro rehab center because I'm a quadriplegic. With all that being said, I still know and believe in my heart that the Lord is with me. I don't worry about how my day, or how my week, or what's going to happen in my life. As long as I can do most of what the Lord wants me to do- if I can be at least half of what He wants from me, I know He's got my back. So I want to ask you, how is your day today? Are you thankful that you woke up? Are you thankful for what you're able to see? Are you thankful for everything the Lord is providing for you? Everyday that you live and breathe He gives you your daily bread. So once in a while give some of your time to Him. Your Father wants to hear from you, as any good father would. Spend time with Him, tell Him you're thankful, you love Him, and tell Him your problems and concerns. He hears you, and He will listen. Be patient, and He will respond. If you don't want to believe me, just ask around and you'll find that there are many, many people who have experienced the love of God. Why don't you?

Again, I'm Jasper and I'm a minister for the Lord.

September 24, 2015

INSURANCE COMPANIES SUCK

Hello my name is Jasper, and I am a quadriplegic in a NeuroCare facility.

For some time now, there have been two things that are bothering me. One is which the insurance companies in Michigan are constantly trying to do away with the no-fault law. This law enables people with brain injuries, spinal cord injuries, and other injuries to live in the better rehab facilities. It disturbs me to know that if they could they would totally do away with this program and we would have to go to nursing homes and other facilities. Most likely the care at these other places would be well below the standard of care we receive now. The other thing that disturbs me is the insurance companies did get a bill passed, whereas they no longer have to pay for personal outings for the physically challenged. There are a great many people in wheelchairs as a result of an auto injury, being ran over by an automobile, and they need constant assistance, especially with travel. I in particular have suffered since this bill has passed. I belong to a wonderful church, which I attended religiously, but now I can no longer get there because insurance won't pay for my trip. I cannot visit my youngest daughter or my brother, both who live in Detroit. They do not have a way to reach me, and I can no longer reach them. Again, because the insurance won't pay. I have missed a number of engagements I was invited to because I had no way to get there. This is just one example of how people in this country who are greatly in need of help do not receive it simply because of greedy corporations. The insurance companies have the money. They have more than enough to do the job they are required to do, but won't. So my fellow readers, supporters, the wheelchair community, anyone who relies on the insurance paying for your transportation to and from. I strongly urge you to contact any political ties that you may have and voice your opinion on this issue. We have people lobbying at the state capital, we have lawyers who are constantly fighting for our rights, and we must show support to them, aid them in correcting this wrong. Remember- the baby that cries the loudest is the one who gets fed first.

Again, my name is Jasper, I'm a quadriplegic, and we're going to make it because we have God on our side and He knows this is not right.

Thank you.

October 15, 2015

TODAY'S LAW ENFORCEMENT

Well if you have watched the latest news as long as I have, you know the tragedy that has occurred. A man was allowed to die in custody, as officers did nothing. This doesn't seem to be happening in one particular area, but it's nationwide. There was a time when you could go to a law officer and you would be relieved to have him help you, but it seems in today's society that's not always the case. It's good that we live in such a wonderful technical world. Imagine how many incidents involving police brutality would go unnoticed if there were no cameras. Imagine what would have happened in the Rodney King incident if there were no cameras or videos. Imagine what would have happened in the Malice Green case in Detroit, where he literally had his brains beaten out by two officers over a few stones of crack. At what point does an officer feel that he's crossed a line? There have been many cases documented, caught on film, caught on camera phones, where officers used excessive force on an unarmed man. There was a case not long ago where a man had made it home, pulled in his driveway, when confronted by officers dropped to his knees, and still they shot him down. In cases such as this, when a man is offering no resistance at all, how are these officers able to explain away their actions? From what I can see, this issue isn't getting better. It seems to be happening more often. To think with all we have accomplished in the world, we still here in 2015 have to fear being slain by an irate police officer. The court system works for you, but it can also work against you. The courts are so overcrowded, there's so much favoritism in the law enforcement industry, that sometimes innocent men go to prison for most of their lives. While people such as a man in Detroit, who exhibited road rage by beating a 21 year old woman, and when approached by onlookers he produced a gun. Further investigation into this matter shows that this felon has had 3 prior arrests for carrying a gun. He also had a knife, which was illegal for him, and he had some assault charges pending against him. My question is, why was he even allowed back on the streets? It is people like this being let out of jail on small infractions in the law, and a woman could have lost her life. These people don't care about human life, or respect, or how much pain they can inflict on another human being. So I want to ask- what is wrong with our law enforcement in this country? I have one theory I would like to offer. You may not understand it, you surely may not believe it, but Satan has very little time left before he has to go into the pit. So he and all his evil spirits are doing a lot of damage in the world today. Just take a look at it and try to understand. Families fighting against each other. Young teenage girls strung out on dope. Old men molesting and raping little boys and girls. Talk of wars and rumors of wars all over the world. All the natural disasters happening in the world today. Neighbor afraid of neighbor. You hustle inside your home and quickly lock the door, pull down the shades, and pray that you will be alright throughout the night. People are scared and, well, they should be. Because if you don't know Jesus and what He can do for you, I feel sorry for you.

My name is Jasper, I love you and keep praying.

October 27, 2015

THE ART OF SHARING

Hello my name is Jasper, and I am a minister for the Lord, and I do his will. The world is turning colder and colder. People are not interested in what the Lord has commanded. Just as the Lord said, man will go their own way. They want to do their dirt in darkness, but the Lord is the light of the world. When you get closer to the Lord, it causes you to take a closer look at yourself. Man's Hart has been waxed cold, men have become lover's of themselves. But the Lord has said, if your brother thirst give him drink, if he hunger, give him food, and if he's cold give him your coat. Father God our creator, wants us to live life with love. JESUS has commanded that we are to love one to another just as he loved us. If you see your brother in need, don't look the other way, stop and help him. We as ministers for the Lord are to help the widow, be a father to the fatherless, we must give of ourselves even if it hurts. This is what the Lord did for us, and we are to follow his example. He suffered for us, and when we feel a little discomfort, we want to stop going. The Lord our God has laid down his commands, and he said, to follow me you must first deny yourself. How many of us are willing to do that? My name is Jasper, and I love you.

November 24, 2015

WHAT DO YOU SEE?

Hello to all my brother and sister in Christ Jesus. I was watching the news, and the things I saw seemed unreal. Isis the terrorists group, are just commenting murder. I watched the Congress discuss what should be done, It seemed to me, they don't know what to do. I watched the story of a young man who was a police officer, and he brutalized a man over a traffic stop. He tried to justify his actions by saying the man was resisting. A video proved that he was lying. There was a case here in Macomb County, where officers literally watched a man die, simply because he did not have his medication. The seasons are not the same as I remembered as a boy. I can remember that in the summer, it was so hot, you didn't want to come outside. In the winter months, you could always be sure to have a lot of snow. Now you still have roses blooming in the cold. There are wars going on all around the world. People are becoming more and more afraid of terrorism. The Lord told his disciples, that man would turn their backs on GOD and become lover's of themselves. People don't seem to care about each other the way they used to. One thing that the Lord is totally against is homosexuality, but as you can see, it is on the rise more than ever. Just open your eyes, then open your Bible, study his word, then tell me what do you see. May the good Lord bless us all. I watched the news, as they told how a four year old boy was maled to death by pit Bulls. I know things happen in life, but can't you see the world has become so cold. Satan is trying to make us kill ourselves, as many as he can. GOD is going to get tired of our sinful ways, and when he chasties us, it will not be pretty. May God bless you and give you his grace.

December 20, 2015

WELL WHAT'S ON YOUR MIND?

Hello to all my brothers and sisters in Christ Jesus. I pray that you had a very blessed Thanksgiving, and ate well and shared much love. The Father is so good to us through his son, our Lord. I hope that you took the time from enjoying his bounty, to give thanks. Sometimes we can get wrapped up in our own pleasures and issues that we can forget about the Lord. But we as followers of the Lord, must stay focused. When you take your eyes off the Lord, your life will slowly begin to sink, like Peter did on the water. When we walk with him, we feel strong in spirit, clear in our thoughts, filled with the spirit of love, and motivated to move forward. The Christmas holiday season is here, and we all know how the world thinks of Christmas. They don't want to celebrate the birth of baby Jesus, they could care less. All they're concerned about is looking good, how much money they've spent. They will take pleasure in decorating their homes and big trees to impress their friends. We must be vigilant and committed to the Lord. We are in the world, but not of the world. As followers of Christ, we are set apart from the world, we have to learn not to do as they do. Follow and thrust in his commandments, don't lose sight of your faith. The Christmas season is here, what's on your mind?

December 23, 2015

WHERE WILL YOU BE WHEN HE COMES BACK?

Hello my name is Jasper, there is a lot of tension in the world today. I am not a racist, and I try my best not to judge others, I try as best I can to help people if I can. I pray that my words will cause you to see this world as I see it. The Lord Jesus told his disciples, that in the last days, people would not fear the Lord anymore. Instead they will go their own way only caring about themselves. They will be lovers of money and their hearts will be waxed cold. I did some sort of drug most of my adult life. When I reflect on my life the way I live today, I can hardly believe that I was that kind of man during those years. But it taught me that if you (allow) the enemy to rule over you, he will take you lower than you ever thought you would go. I am trying to get a point over to my brothers and sisters that if you are not in line with GOD, you need to so. The world is not going to get better, its getting worse. Police shooting unarmed (kids), you can hardly stop at a gasoline station without fearing for your life. Our senior citizens being preyed upon with no mercy. He also said that there would be wars and rumors of wars. He also said that there would be great pleages upon the land, and we now have diceses that have no cure. I have found out something that you are going to find out too, if you don't already know. There is only one way to live your life the way the Lord intended, totally submit to HIM. Remember, you cannot serve two masters. I love you my brothers and sisters in Christ Jesus.

December 29, 2015

BEING SAVED

Being Saved is the same as you being in the river and the current is dragging you down, then someone throws a rope to you, and pulls you to safety. You have just been (saved) from a horrible death. Your life was spared because someone cared enough to (save) you. Well that's what the Father did for us, when he sent his only begotten son to die for us. Father God was angry with us because of our sinful lives. He could not find one sinless man on earth. But because of his love for us, he made a way out for us. He sent the Lamb of God , to take on our sins and diceses, all the vile that was in us, HE took it to the cross with HIM, where it died with HIM.HE did it out of love for us, that is why Jesus is love, and all HE wants from us is to love our fellow man just as HE loved us. Stop our sinful ways and confess that HE is Lord. Learn how to worship HIM and follow HIS commandments. Being saved is not an event, its a lifestyle that a lot of people are not ready for yet. Serving the Lord requires a lot more than just sitting in church every Sunday. Do you pay your thiths as you should, do you pray and pray often (not just on Sunday), do you pray for people and not just yourself? Do you help the widow who has nobody? Are you a father to those without father's, and are you willing to help someone you don't know, just because they need help? These are just some of the requirements of being a good Christian. Tell me, have you even thought of GOD today? If he were here what would you say? Show someone some love today, help someone along the way. May GOD bless my brothers and sisters in Christ.

2016

January 10, 2016

LIFE IS GOOD

Hello saints of GOD, may the Lord always bless you. I used to live a very sin filled life. I reflect on how I lived my life every day for the enemy, and how he kept me down and in misery. The Lord had blessed me with a wonderful young wife, and eventually a beautiful family. But I didn't know anything about how to deal with the tricks he would throw at me. I began to hang out all night with all kinds of women, doing drugs. I reached a point to where I began to spend all my money in the streets. I neglected my home, my job, and my friends. I lost my self respect, didn't care about me or any one else. My life had become a confusing mess for me. I didn't know what to do, I would not listen to anyone. But the Lord still loved me even though I didn't deserve it. He gave me all kinds of opportunities to help myself, but I was so stubborn and the enemy had me so bound up. The Lord had plans for me, and HIS will shall be done, no matter what. I had survived three near fatal car crashes. The second one I lost my wife, and still I would commit willful sins. I truly believe that the Lord just chastised me to save my life. I could have died out there on 1-94 that night, breaking my neck. But my Lord would not let me die. I became a quad and I began to get close to my Lord. I believe that He had a different plan for my life, but first I had to slow down, get right in my spirit. He slowed me down to give me time to see life clearly. I began to truly see just how good HE has been to me. The best day of my life was when I asked Him to be Lord of my life. There is only one way to live your life the way it should be, and that is in the care of the Lord. Take time to go to your quiet place and think about just how wonderful the Lord is to us. My name is Jasper, and I pray that you are doing well and happy in God's care. Much love to you saints of GOD.

January 28, 2016

GRATITUDE

Hello my name is Jasper, and may the Lord bless the readers of my blogs. The Lord has been so good to us for so long, how could we ever forget to give him his glory. He loved us before we were even formed in our mothers womb. He loved us when HE spoke our lives into existence and continued to love us as we sinned and made a mess of our blessing. While we were yet sinners, HE suffered for us. Even as far as taking our sins and vile lives, even our diceses to the cross, so that we could have a right to life. What an awesome and loving GOD we serve, the only true and everlasting GOD. Thank you Lord, Thank you Lord for you are so worthy of our praise. I appeal to you my brothers and sisters in Christ, take the time out of your day, to spend some time with GOD. Show HIM that you truly love HIM and you are his servant. I make it a habit to tell HIM thank you Lord, for opening my eyes, so that I can see another day I've never seen before. I thank God for this blessing called life and for every hardship I have endured to learn how to live it HIS way. I tried for a long time to live life my way. I always knew who the Lord was, but I wasn't going to be one of those church going Christian hipicrits. Not being connected to the true vine, the enemy took hold of me, and caused me to sink lower than I ever thought I could. My life soon fell apart, I was just a walking mess, alone, hurt, confused, and not one clue about what to do. But my Lord, my master, did not forsake me. HE took care of me in the middle of my chaos, and guided my steps towards HIM, thank you oh my Lord. Through the Lord's will, I have survived three near fatal car crashes. But the last one in which I broke my neck is the one that I'm thankful for. Although it put me in a wheelchair and a rehabilitation center, I became closer to the Lord than I've ever been before. So you see I am very GRATEFUL for his rod of correction. I know I have favor with the Lord, for scripture says, HE only chastises those who HE loves. I thank you Lord always for saving my gift called life. Saints of GOD may you always be blessed, and never forget to show HIM your GRATITUDE ☺ LOVE you all.

February 24, 2016

ARE YOU READY?

Hello to my brothers and sisters in Christ, I greet you in his holy name. May the Lord continue to bless you and keep you. I don't watch the news often, but I did last night. I have heard some people say that they prefer not to watch the news, now I can see why. It's full of some depressing acts of violence which make no sense at all. A man, for no apparent reason took a pistol and shot people at random. He managed to kill six, and injured two. A man is responsible for the death of a mother and her daughter. A four year old girl was shot in the head by a stray bullet. Four young kids brought a gun to school, with the intention of shooting some other kids. My brothers and sisters I want to remind you that, Satan said his greatest feat was convincing the world that he doesn't exist. But as you look at what's going on in the world, how can we deny it. The devil is as a roaring lion, roaming around seeking whomever he may devour. The Lord spoke of spirits and demonic spirits that will ruin our lives if you don't know Jesus. Demonic spirits are afraid of His very name, and He tells us how to deal with them in His holy name. Murder, greed, families fighting with each other, racial hatetred, crooked politicians, fear everywhere. We are living in the last days, and Satan's behind it all. But he will never win, because He that lives in me is greater than he that is in the world. The Lord defeated Satan when He gave himself to the cross. He bought us with HIS precious blood. We should always remember who we are, and whose we are and know that He is Lord. Ask yourself this question, when the Lord comes for his people, are you ready? Have you been living a righteous life, and having love for your brother as the Lord commanded? Or do you only think of yourself and your needs. Well don't worry about it, He will judge your lifestyle and the way you judged others. He said in His word, if you love me, you will keep my commandments. This is just something to think about, if He came back right now, are you ready? My name is Jasper, may the Lord have mercy.

March 1, 2016

THE OSCAR'S

Hello to my brothers and sisters in Christ. Once again I watched the world show just how one sided it can be, creating a problem. It all came about when there were no people of color nominated for any categories, even though there were black movies that were worthy. This sparked anger with some of the leading black actors, and they boycotted the Oscar's. Now this tells me to remember who is the author of confusion and unrest, Satan. I would take a guess and believe a lot of those millionaires are not connected to the Lord. I don't care who you are or how high you think you have reached, if you don't know the Lord, the enemy will come in and create chaos. Those people cannot overlook their brothers and sisters as if they don't exist, or not worthy enough for you. When you treat your own brother and sister wrong, this will surely bring the enemy your way. We as a nation of people must learn to love and support each other the way the Lord commanded, or it's all going to unravel. The Lord intended for all his children to love each other, respect, support, and be your brothers keeper. If we can never learn to do this, well when HE comes back, all I can say is, I'm glad I have a relationship with the Master. His judgment of the unrighteous will be swift and terrible. Peace and love to you and may the Lord always bless you and your family. Hello my name is Jasper.

March 8, 2016

THINGS I'VE LEARNED AT NCC

Hello my name is Jasper and I am a quadriplegic, and I pretty much have no use of my body. You may view this as the worst thing that could happen to you, well not so. Never give up or give in, keep a strong positive attitude, and above all don't forget whose running things. I don't know how you may look at your situation, but my accident changed my mind set and out look on life. When I first arrived at NCC, I was emotionly bankrupt, I was isolated in my room all the time. I would not participate in anything, and I was constantly on the pity pot. I didn't start to grow until I realized that life is truly a gift from God. Yours may not be the way you want it, but life is not over for you my friend. In fact, depending on your attitude, you could be on your way to a life you never thought you could have. First you realize that God saved you for a reason, and helping people with a loving heart, good things will come to you. I'm telling you from my own experience, my accident brought me closer to the Lord than I've ever been. Slowly things started to open up for me. By being friendly with a positive spirit I soon knew everyone by first name. I took the initiative to learn new things, and to try my best to upgrade myself. The world does not stop because I'm in a wheelchair. You have a choice to sit and do nothing, or look past your circumstances and become a member of society once again. I make it a practice to attend any (sci) spinal cord injury meeting. I'ts where I can learn about new programs and services that are designed to help us. They discuss how we can do things that other people do such as driving, traveling with a wheelchair, sky diving, driving boats, and much more. Also some of us may believe that for us relationships and sex is over, but that's not true. At the (sci) meetings we discuss adaptive equipment that enables us to have sex. There are also pills and other medical procedures to aid us. I've also learned by living at NCC, just how blessed I am that I'm still alive, I can see and talk and think for myself. I see people every day that have no idea what is going on around them, or can't control any part of their bodies. It should humble you and make you realize how blessed you are. I pray that you understand the point I'm trying to make to you my brothers and sisters that are in wheelchairs. My name is Jasper and much love to you.

March 29, 2016

STUDY HIS WORD

Hello to all my brothers and sisters in Christ. May the Lord always bless you and your family. I pray that my words come straight from the spirit of the Lord that lives in me. We as children of God, are obligated to study our fathers commands, so that we become children HE will be proud of. Jesus said "if you love me you will keep my commandments".Also HIS words act as a guide as well as a shield against the evil one.I was invited to join in on a bible study by a friend, and I thought it would be a good idea. At first the studying seem to be fine. By the time we were going to end our studying, the teaching began to change. He stated some things that we don't teach where I worship and learn the word. Jesus said that, HIS followers must not be deceived when others come with false doctrine. In order to keep your head on straight, you must know your word because they will confuse you with good sounding doctrine. I found myself in this situation and it began to vex my spirit (thank you holy ghost). We must always be on the lookout for the enemy, who is constantly looking for a way in. His only job is to keep your mind off the word of God. He hates us because GOD made us in his image, and HE loves us even more than the angels in heaven. So be a good disciple for the Lord so when you have to stand before HIM, HE will say "well done my good and faithful servant. Thank you and may GOD BLESS!

April 5, 2016

STATE OF EMERGENCY!

Hello my name is Jasper and I want to call your attention to the conditions, that we are currently living under. Saints of GOD, we can't afford to turn a deaf ear to this, nor a blind eye. He that lives in me is greater than he that lives in the world. With that in mind, we the church should stand steadfast whenever we see evil in the world. Remember that the Lord said we can do all things through Christ Jesus, who will give us strength, knowledge, and the shield of his precious blood. The world right now is in a state of emergency, and only the Lord can save us. Thanks my brothers and sisters in Christ, God Bless.

April 26, 2016

BABY KILLERS

Hello my name is Jasper, and I send you my love and my prayers. My brothers and sisters in Christ, we must come from out of our comfort zones and stand up for what is right. Each one of us is not only a minister for the Lord, we must be the light in this dark world. The fight may belong to Jesus, but we're his foot soldiers, fighting in the trenches for the Lord. He told us in his word that "I can do ALL things through Christ Jesus who strengthens me". Against my better judgment, I will watch the news and all you see is murder, mistreatment of people, fear, genocide abroad, and chaos in our own communities. The Lord will be back one day, because he said He would, and He is a God that cannot lie. When He does he is going to set everything in order. I pray that you have your business straight with the Lord, because if you don't, when He comes back it will be too late. Stand for what you know He stands for, what He gave himself to the cross for. When you gave your life to the Lord, you made a commitment to obey his word. His words are not to hide in fear and do nothing. So search your hearts and spirit, pray for God to guide you, and may the Lord always bless you. AMEN

May 12, 2016

A BEAUTIFUL WORLD, OUT OF CONTROL

Hello to my brothers and sisters in Christ Jesus, I greet you with much love and blessings. I pray that you are doing well and the Lord is the focus of your life. I love you, and I prayed before I began to write, because I have this feeling inside of me I long to give to you. I pray that the message I hope to relate, touches someone who may be hurting and afraid to say. Touches someone who Satan has all bound up in something they can't handle, as he once had me. I pray that this message be inspired by the will of God, and will cause someone to stand up and declare that the Lord be the head of their life. My brothers and sisters I encourage you to reach out to the weak spirits and teach them to be strong. Take the time to help guide a young person to the right path. The world is turning colder and colder every day, shootings, car jackings, robbery, rape, our babies being killed in their own front yards. We as God's elect, must pray harder and longer, to come against these evil spirits. We are not merely church goers trying to convince ourselves we are good Christians. For if you are, well stop fooling yourself today, God sees what's in your heart. There is no fooling Him, hiding from Him, or out running Him. And one day you, me, and everyone will have to answer to what we did, or didn't do. We are in a spiritual warfare like it or not, and the Lord gives us free will to choose our side. I choose to be on the side of the Lord, I've learned some, and I'm still learning His word. The world is out of control, and the saints must be the Beacon of light that guides the unsaved to Jesus. We have to show the world by example that strength, love, peace, joy, and salvation can only come by Christ. May the Lord continue to bless you and your family. PEACE AND LOVE, AMEN!!

June 7, 2016

THE WORLD AND KATELYN JENNER

Hello my brothers and sisters in Christ my name is Jasper, and may the Lord always bless you. I just wanted you to pay attention to the things that the world thinks is important. Jesus said that most of the things that the world does is nonsense and it vexes his spirit. I was watching a television program, and they were focusing on the year Bruce Jenner was an Olympic Champion. He was glorified as the epitamy of manhood, a male icon for America. He was blessed with many lucrative endorsements, personal appearances, and so on. But now all of that is history as far as Bruce is concerned, his desire is to become a woman. To change the very nature of what the Lord made him to be. The Lord has declared that the Father frowns on what is unnatural. Those who choose to participate in the unnatural such as homosexuality, sex with children or animals, masturbation, whoremonglers, etc. But in the last day's it is written that man will turn away from God and go their own way. They will be consumed with their own devices, lovers of themselves only, greedy, puffed up with pride. That's why Bruce Jenner, who is now Katelyn Jenner is looked upon as a trailblazer. Gracing the covers of top magazines, receiving all kinds of awards. The world has little or no respect for the word of God. We the church must pray and stand up for what we know is right. Thank you and GOD bless you.

June 16, 2016

TERRORISM IS IN AMERICA

Hello my name is Jasper and I greet you in his holy name. I pray that the words that I write today, are blessed by the Lord. We are truly living in the last day's, and evil is on the rise. Our young people are killing each other at an alarming rate. Car jackings, rape, our babies being killed in their own front yards. Murder in our schools and school officials stealing money from our kids. The church must pray against these evils, and stand firm in our belief in His holy word. We should be that shining light of hope for the world to see. The Lord shed His precious blood for us, saving us for times such as this, so we can carry His message to the unsaved. Saints I encourage you to pray, pray, and pray harder for the victims in Orlando. Pray and don't judge, because we are all children of God. We must learn to love each other, but we don't have to condone the sinful act that a person may do. What happened in Orlando was a tragedy, and those victims were someone's son, daughter, parent, loved one, etc, etc, and etc. My heart, thoughts and prayers go out to the families of the fallen victims. It should not matter what their lifestyle was, God gave us all free will, and they will have to answer to the Lord, not us. He gave us the freedom to live as we choose and if you choose not to obey Him, you will have face the judgement. I also urge you to send out your prayers, for the young woman from the show, The Voice who was slain in cold blood. Evil spirits turned a man into a tool of death, and he cut short the life of a young woman who had a bright future. I know the pain of anyone who has suffered the loss of a loved one to murder. We don't always understand, but I trust in the Lord and He doesn't make mistakes. I pray that my words will cause you to search your heart, and find love and compassion for the less fortunate. All praise and glory to the Lord. Love and peace to you all.

July 9, 2016

LISTEN TO GOD

Hello to my brothers and sisters in Christ, my name is Jasper, and I greet you in his holy name. I pray that you are doing well and happy. I also pray that you are paying attention to the things that are going on in the world. Don't allow yourself to get so distracted that you don't notice the horrible things that SATAN is doing. We, God's people must pray hard for those poor innocent victims murdered by the police. We need to also pray hard for our innocent babies that are being killed by reckless gunfire. We are killing each other over things that don't really matter. The people that shot into a car killing that child, just because they were asked to stop with the fireworks and go home. The police seem have gone berserk the way they have been behaving, and its all across the country. You're almost afraid to pull over these days for fear of your life. The way that young man was murdered in front of his fiance after he announced he had a legal firearm, and was reaching for his license and paperwork. There are many accounts where the police shot UNARMED citizens, and got away with it. You may feel anger in your mind, but we have to remember and listen to the word of God. Vengeance is mine so saieth the Lord. We have to be reminded that GOD is still on the throne, and the world is his, HE will do as HE sees fit. AMEN. Our goal is to listen to the word, be obedient, and be the shining light of the Lord, for all the world to see. Our job is to be the example of the Lord, and be his ministers to those in need. We must believe that HE will administer justice to this unsaved world. Glory to the Lord for keeping us, and praise him for what HE has already done. Peace and love to you always my brothers and sisters in Christ. Again my name is Jasper and I love you all. AMEN.

October 24, 2016

STAND UP AND GET COUNTED

Hello to my brothers and sisters in Christ. I pray that you are doing well and blessings are coming your way. Dear Lord, I pray that every thought and word that springs fourth from my mouth, comes from you. The world seems to be getting more unrighteous with each day, they are only concerned with themselves and have little or no respect for anyone else. But we that are deeply rooted in Christ, must speak out against the evil we see. With nothing but faith, and the Lord's word, be his lamps in a dark and cold world. We have to show the world it's good to help someone, it is ok to walk away from the drama, It's a good thing to pick up a bible, read and let the Lord embrace you. The news today is filled with confusion, murder, our babies are being killed, car jackings and home invasions. We know that we are blessed to be covered by the precious blood of our Lord. The Lord we serve wants us to be an example to the unsaved, the same way He was an example to those who wish to follow Him. I know that I pray that I can be a blessing to someone today. I can minister to someone who is hurting inside. I pray that the Lord would use me to help console a heavy heart. So my family in Christ Jesus, love you all and my prayers are with you.

2017

April 4, 2017

NEVER GIVE UP

GREETINGS my brothers and sisters in Christ, I Pray that our LORD has shone favor to you. He is a loving God that gives us grace, knowing we don't deserve it. Take a thought on how the LORD wants us to behave, then think on how we do behave. HE said love each other, not to murder, steal cheat, and lie the way we do. The scripture says that we are to be meek and lowly, slow to anger, quick to understand. we are to the world, strange and peculiar people because we live our lives by a different code of conduct. We don't react to things the way the world does. We follow the LORD, and obey his word, and trust that he will guide our steps. Living in our Christian life can be very painful at times, but we know that the outcome is worth it. The point I want to make is, pray, pray, pray, and have faith, because it is impossible to please GOD without faith. We have to reach a point where we see something out of place, or someone in spiritual pain, and we learn to minister to that person. The world is at a place where it's plane to see that it's good against evil. Everywhere you go now, people are afraid of getting hurt or worse. We can't allow the enemy to shut down our lives and shake our faith. Fight the enemy just as Jesus fought him with scriptures and solid faith. If you have not set your affairs in line with the Lord ...I suggest you do so. AMEN

MAY 9, 2017

BELIEVE IN HIM

Hello my brothers and sisters in Christ Jesus, I have something on my mind I want to share with you. I'm a quad.,so I take life very seriously. My life is a precious gift
given to me by my heavenly father.Believe that your being born at that particular time, year, month, day, hour and so on,was no fluke, it was all planned by the Father. I'm talking
about things you can't touch, see, hear, or smell. Still you must believe that they exist, the new testament speaks of them often. When you give your life to Lord Jesus, and learn just who he is and what He did for you and me,He will open your eyes. You will understand the evil things that are in the world today, that the word of Jesus was true way back then, and how to protect yourself through His word.Lots,and lots
of the things Jesus said would come true are in the world today. Man would turn his back on GOD, homosexuality
would be considered normal to man, man would have little or no regard for his fellow man. The love of money would
take over a mans mind and make his heart cold. Man would
eliminate the word of GOD anyway he can, in the schools
in the corporate world, in the news media and radio. The
threat of war is always present, I urge you to get your affairs straight with the Lord, because nobody knows

when He
will return, but He will.Goodbye and peace be with you.

June 5, 2017

GOD IS LOVE

Hello my brothers and sisters in Christ Jesus, I pray that your life and mind is centered in the body of Christ. Think on this, if you are having a lot of grief, confusion, unrest, and hard times, you need Jesus in your life. I always knew who he was, but I didn't know what he was to my life. I didn't have a clue that Jesus is love and why he had to die so that I could live. Some people say they don't believe he is real and alive, but I know that he is. I'm a quad,I've had lots of time to reflect on my life and I can see that Satan had me bound up and hurt, but my lord set me free and saved me from a life of sin. It's a great feeling to know my GOD love me yesterday, today, tomorrow and evermore. As long as I keep my eyes on HIM, I have nothing to fear. He will do for me what I can't do for myself. He will go to the Father on my behalf and speak my name with love and compassion. His love for me will keep the enemy from me, my family, and people I care for. I love you master, I worship you, I give you praise for you are so worthy of all praise. With you as my Lord, I know I am truly blessed. He said He was going away to prepare a place in paradise for us, to be with Him. I urge you my brothers and sisters to get your affairs straight with the Lord, He is HOLY and cannot lie. He said He will be back and you don't want to miss the second coming of the LORD,You really don't. Much love and peace to you.

June 17, 2017

STOP, LOOK, LISTEN TO THE LORD

Hello to my family in Christ Jesus, I pray that He has truly blessed you. My name is Jasper and I know all to well how Satan will destroy your life, but only if you allow Him to. It took me a long time to come to the Lord, and to understand that it was Him that saved me. Slowly he took me apart and I didn't see it because I didn't know the Lord like I do today praise the Lord. My life became a total wreck, drug addiction, separated from the people who love me, and set apart from my family. Just as it says in the scriptures, you must stay connected to the true vine or you'll be separated and all alone. If you find yourself apart from the Lord, The enemy will have his way with you. No matter what you think, we ourselves can't handle Satan. We need the power of the Lord, his word, strong faith, and unwavering loyalty to the Lord to see us through. Sometimes we run here and there trying to do God's job only to burn ourselves out, become frustrated and confused and spiritruly bankrupt. The Lord told us that the battle is not ours, and his arms are open wide to receive us. Just let go of everything and put on his yoke, for it is easy and light. He loves us and promised to always be with us, even to the end of time, watching over us. Sometimes just stop and take a good long look at your life. Examine how you got to where you are, close your eyes and listen for that soft whispering voice. In times such as these we must learn to worship our Lord the God of LOVE. Goodbye my brothers and sisters, love one another and remain steadfast in the faith.

June 22, 2017

ALL ABOUT HATE

Hello, my name is Jasper and I have an opinion about a subject that has been around for decades. What I'm speaking of are issues involving race, stereotypes, and racial profiling. I find it hard to accept that after all we've seen, been through, suffered, and lost, we still want to hate because of color. Its not just an American black and white issue anymore, its all over the world. People committed to ethnic cleansing, police shooting after shooting for no logical reason. To make matters even worse, we now have a leader talking about hitting people in the face if they don't agree with you. He will insult women, people of color, and anyone of a different culture. In this world today, we should embrace each other, not building walls between people. Being a committed servant of our Lord Christ Jesus, I must say, too many people are being ruled by the enemy, Satan. A lot of people don't understand nor believe in the spiritual world because they can't see or touch. But all the things that are happening in the world today were told to us thousands of years ago by Jesus himself. I'm in no way trying to push my beliefs and thoughts on anyone, that is just one of the things that makes this country great. You have the right to express yourself as you see fit. I'm waiting for the day to come where people will understand that life is a precious thing and that hate is just wrong. Again my name is Jasper and I love you.

July 3, 2017

GOING THROUGH THE STORM

Hello to all the saints of God, may our Lord continue to bless thee and all that you love. As we walk through this thing we call life, its not always smooth or even in our favor. People we thrust may turn away from us, we may be criticized for something we had no hand in. Sometimes the storm can be so overwhelming it seems to just smother our lives. When
we find ourselves in this portion of life, confused, hopeless emotionally and spirituality drained, learn to just stand still and know that He is Lord. The Lord our God is sinless,He
is Love, when we go through the storm he is in there with us. In the Bible, the Holy word of God, He tells us in Matthew that there will be times of longsuffering ,there will be pain and sorrow. But to count it all joy because crying will last throughout the night, but joy comes in the morning. We
may go into the rough times but keep steadfast your faith, don't waver to the left nor the right. History of Moses,Joshua, Daniel and the lions den David and King Saul,the three
Hebrew boys and the furnace. These are some examples of hard times, but through faith and obedience,the Lord brought all of them through. He is still doing today what He did back then, work miracles in our lives. Amen and may God bless.

July 24, 2017

SURVIVING THE DAY

First I must give all thanks and praise to our Lord, Jesus the Christ. Without you I would be helpless against the evil one. Lord you are my strength and my total salvation. My name is Jasper, and I've learned that every day is a blessing from you, and you use me as you see fit. I have absolutely no use of my body, so each day I don't like to waste. I fill my day by being that lamp for the Lord, people should see Him in me. The calmness, the confidence, joy, contentment, love, and caring. When there is unrest and chaos, you are calm because you are set apart from the rest of the world. People should see peace in the midst of the storm and the spirit of the Lord should come from you. You have realized that He who lives in you, is greater than he that is in the world. You represent the Kingdom of the Lord, walking upright, praying for those who won't pray for themselves, praying constantly for the unsaved.
Showing love to all of those who are around you.I try as best as I can to do His will, and that fills my day with joy. I don't know what you think about your life each day,but if you feel that there is something missing, join us in building up the Kingdom. This is Jasper and love from above be with you.

AUGUST 1, 2017

WHAT A WONDERFUL WORLD

Hello to you and praise God for His mercy. I have to admit using a laptop computer is all new to me. But it is a beautiful thing to have in our world today. I like to get on the laptop and go all around the world and see the different customs and experience the culture. I have been looking at the people of Brazil, and I must say they are very vibrant. Also the landscapes are just incredible. They also have some of the best beaches in the world. There is a dark
side to this heavenly paradise. They are pledged with poverty and ghettos. For a lot of the men, there is no work, so they turn to drug trafficking. The rich and well to do, guard themselves from that side of Rio.Still it remains to be one of the best vacation spots in the world. Now along with Rio,I checked out a bit of the land down under. They too have a strong and very spicy night life.
So when you take that fantasy vacation, don't forget about these two places.

August 24, 2017

MY LIFE IN A REHAB

Hello to whoever is reading this, especially to those who are believers in the Lord. I wanted to start my message this way, because I believe He placed me here. It is only by the will of God I bought the insurance when I did, otherwise I would not be at special tree today. He knew I would need coverage but I didn't. Just as I didn't know that on April 28 09 ,my entire life was going to change. The world that I knew would cease to exist, and I was introduced to the world of a different kind, that of a quadtrapaligic.I have always been the type of man that was spontaneous, now I need 24 hour care because my body is of no use to me . But I thank God for saving my life, and guiding my daughters to special tree, a place none of us knew anything about. Through the years I've come to understand that, it is one of the best rehabilitation facilities in the state of Michigan. When I gave my children the task of finding a rehab for dad, they had three in mind. But what truly caught their interest in special tree was the way the V.P.Jack knew most of the clients by name. They told me aside from being very clean, it had a
family feel to it. The staff consisted of a lot of young women who in my opinion, do a job most people could not do, Taking care of a person who cannot do for themselves, is not as easy as you may think. Cleaning up after a person who has soiled the bed and themselves, takes a lot of caring. Trying to help dress a person, or shower them, even getting them to eat can turn into a nightmare. What the Lord was showing me was, when you have good health, family and friends

that care,each day you open your eyes, it is a blessing. You don't have to die to have your life taken from you. Being at the tree has shown me just how fragile life can be. Take a minute or two and give thanks for keeping me safe last night, and then opening my eyes to see a new day. They told me that I was bruised and hostile when I first arrived here. I went through a series of emotions and different levels of acceptance. I also had bouts with being in denial,which will keep you stuck emotionally. But thank the Lord that the staff knew right where I was, and they let me be me until I was ready to change. They didn't try to pressure me, but slowly
brought me out of my shell. I began to be a little more open with people, and the activities department played a big role in my rehabilitation. A lot of the games and activities that they offered, I never got into so I wasn't interested.

August 30, 2017

THE PROPHECY

Hello to my brothers and sisters in Christ, I greet you in His holy name. I stopped watching so much news, because it can be depressing. I still hear things that are happening and it reminds me of scriptures. I remember reading what Jesus told his followers when they asked him, what will happen in the last days. He told them a few things to look out for at this time. Men will turn their backs on GOD, they will try to erase the name Jesus from as many things as they can. They took prayer out of our schools, courts, and many institutions. They don't want you to talk of Jesus in some places, for fear it may offend some people. He also spoke of men being lovers of themselves, hearts being waxed cold. Men having no love or empathy for their fellow man. There will be wars and rumors of war. Silly women will take no good men into their homes. You may not be able to tell one season from another, and that chaos will be in many places. I urge you to take heed to what is happening in the world today, and then read it in your family bible. If you are not a believer in Christ, I understand but at least read, research and compare your findings. This particular time in the world which we are entering, is called " the beginning of sorrows". There is so much evil going on, how could you not believe. Children murdering their parents, raping little children, Isis committing genocide. As true believers, we must stand against this evil. I am Jasper, may the LORD bless you.

2021

May 19, 2021

MY LAST BLOG POST

Hello my brothers and sisters. It's your brother, Jasper Matthews again. Sorry it's been so long since I wrote to you. I'm in hospice care now. It's been a long journey but I have reached a point where no more can be done for me medically. I just have to ride the time out in hospice until the end. Now let me say this- you and I don't know when the end might be. I have felt close to the end of my time, and I tried to rush it with medicine, silence, being withdrawn from everything. It seemed as though God would let me go all the way to the end of the cliff and pull me back, not letting me fall. A strange feeling that you're going to God and then you don't. I have so many besides my family coming by and wishing me well, to touch me and love me, send me their well-wishes. and I felt I was letting them down by not dying. My preacher once told me "you won't know until Father God calls you home. He may come close many times, feeling like it's your time, and then you come back to full recovery." So, if any one of you is going through something similar to this just hang on. You may feel like you're going to have your last day, your last moment, your last breath, but not so. Only He can call you home. A great relief. I agree with one nurse I was speaking with when I told her I hate drifting off to sleep because I wake up and I have anxiety. and it scares me. and I said I don't know why I'd be scared. Maybe it's because I don't know what's on the other side. People get scared to leave this world and go to the other side because we have a great fear of the unknown. We don't know what to expect on the other side so we draw back, like I do. She said that's it. We don't know what's on the other side, so that's why we get scared. But when the end comes you'll know. You won't question, you'll just know. Some folks even say you'll hear your father call you. He'll say "come home" like the sermon. He'll say "come home, my Son, and rest". That in itself is scary, but it's something we all have to go through. I made it to a point in time to live, and a point in time to die. Well, I'm going to continue on with my hospice care. Doing the best I can. The staff is very important. I have felt very blessed. I have been very blessed to have wonderful staff. Caring, loving, supportive, and giving. We are treated like a family. Again, the Lord put me right where I needed to be. I'm around the people I need in my life. My best friend, who understands me has stood by me through the years (well over 50 years as a brother). We've been through so many things together. He understands me, will tell me when I'm wrong, and we know the Lord put us together because no one else understands me like he does. Through all my bad times in life, he understood. He would come and minister to me, pick me up off the ground. When no one else understood, when I was going through drugs, he told me through it all, he saw I was a good person. People tend to shy away from you when they know you're a drug user. They say things about you that aren't true. Well he never did. He would never hesitate to accept me into his home, into his life. He told me he saw the God light in me, and that's what people see. They feel the kindred spirit. They see my spirit, not me. I have been truly blessed in that respect. He said that's why people are drawn to me. Drawn to me because of the spirit they see in me. People I've only met one time come back and see me years later. They always keep plans with me, be concerned for me, and pray for me. I didn't understand why people were drawn to me. I even have a girl in housekeeping here and she'll come by and say "Allah". She can't speak any English. We haven't even had a conversation. But she'll stop what she's doing, stop what she's doing, and say "Allah. I love you. I love you more." I don't know why. I just accept it. It's a beautiful thing. So when people are drawn to you and you can't figure out why, it just may be Jesus' spirit that they see in you. Not you, not the physical. It's the spiritual glow you have inside that draws them to you. Let's them know you're not a bad person.

Acknowledgements

I would like to give a special thanks to the people God put in my life who inspired me to write this book. To my spiritual leaders- Apostle Lee, my pastor, and his lovely wife Apostle Sylvia. To my daughters who told me "Daddy, you should write a book". To Courtney Riehle, who is very inspirational in helping me put this book together as I dictate it to her. To Jennifer Dumouchelle, for helping me publish this book. To my friends that God put in my life who gave me lots of encouragement and inspiration through the years. To all the people that God placed in my life to help me along the way and taught me things when I didn't know I was learning, a special thanks and a special prayer to all of you.

About the Author

I grew up on the East side of Detroit, Michigan. My family migrated to Detroit from Jackson, Mississippi in 1957. I remember my family talking about the "race riot" that was going on when they arrived here. I remember my grandfather saying you could not stop at a red light, you had to just keep going through it. I have memories of growing up on John R street, walking distance to downtown Detroit, and I remember playing at one of the houses where there were always lots of people walking up and down the sidewalks. I grew up in a small family unit mainly my mother, who was divorced from my father, my grandparents, and my older brother. I did not grow up in a household where there was a lot of partying going on, nor were there any drugs, a minimal amount of alcohol was used. Sometimes I might see my mother and my grandfather drinking a beer, but that was the extent of it. So why did I start smoking weed in my early twenties, which escalated to popping pills, and then snorting cocaine, and then the last thing I did was smoke crack. It's almost as if one day I was riding down the street in my Mustang convertible, young and free, and then the next instant I was a crack addict. Not bathing, collecting pop bottles to get food, often sleeping in abandoned houses, lying, selling everything I owned, and estranged from my family. Well, I understand it better now than ever before. That is because getting close to Christ opened my eyes. I can look back at different situations I was in, people I had no business being with, out all hours of the night, and I imagine like most addicts I asked myself "how did I get here?" Even after I came to Christ I asked the question "why would he allow me to be an addict?" Well, we go through life's tough situations to teach us. Sometimes we won't think of Christ until we are backed into a corner, until we have dug a hole so deep it seems no one can get us out. But danger is all about us and we need help and relief. Then He gets us alone where there's nobody but you and Him. Then you're open to receive his word. That is the basis on which I build my book. I know someone reading this book is in pain or confused, don't know which way or who to turn to. It's been my life experience if you turn to Christ, reflect back on your life, you will see that it is Him who kept you out of danger. Kept you out of jail. Stopped you from being killed. And we owe him, which is why I want to give back through this book. I pray the Lord will speak through my book to encourage and empower someone in need.